THE HOME BOOK OF
English Cookery

JOYCE STUBBS

FABER & FABER
3 Queen Square, London

*First published in 1972
by Faber and Faber Limited
3 Queen Square London WC1
Printed in Great Britain by
Latimer Trend & Co Ltd Plymouth*

ISBN 0 571 09937 8

THE HOME BOOK OF
ENGLISH COOKERY

Contents

To the many friends who have so generously given me their family recipes, my grateful thanks.

My thanks also to George Begley, to my publishers and not least to my husband, for their help and patience.

Introduction

While there are fish and chips on the Costa Brava, bacon and eggs in Brussels, 'Rosbif' and 'Englisch pouding' all over the continent, at home we serve Peking Duck, Spaghetti Bolognese, Moussakas, Circassian Chicken and many other dishes encountered abroad.

In spite of all temptations to belong to other nations there is a lot to be said for remaining an English cook. More and more foreigners are realizing as they visit England that although possibly we could provide the world's most comprehensive 'Bad Food Guide' the good English dishes are not only très snob but very eatable. These are not only the classics, roast beef, pork and lamb, but Dickensian items such as sausage and mash, steak and kidney pie, bread-and-butter pudding. Any foreigner who stayed long enough to become bi-culinary would be serving a great many more even in gastronomic citadels such as Dijon. With a touch of national pride, I propose to present a number of them here.

The trouble with hackneyed phrases is that they are so often to the point. I make no apologies for repeating 'there is no bad food, only bad cooks' and this goes for English food in a massive way, or as the food snobs put it, the British housewife usually empties the best of the dish down the sink. Why?

The truth is that some of the most admirable food—as well as some of the worst—is obtainable in England. The food has to be good in itself and well cooked or else it is plain dull or even horrible. Whereas in other countries cooks enliven their

7

dishes with garlic and spices, the British approach lets the dish
depend on the quality of the materials and the dedication of
the cook.

If the formulas are: put it in the oven and it's roasted, drop
it in hot fat and it's fried, plunge it in boiling water and throw
the goodness away with the water, then 'result misery' as Mr.
Micawber used to say. On the other hand, watch the meat
vigilantly till it is done to a turn, make the gravy by swilling
some of the vegetable cooking liquid round the tin combining
the juices of the meat with the flavour of fresh vegetables—
result: happiness.

'Food like mother used to make' is a recurrent nightmare
for many wives. My husband still maintains that the only place
for rice is in a pudding, and my meat and potato pie will never
be as good as those he ate in his formative years. The object
of this book is not to provide a complete handbook on English
cooking but to describe the preparation of a representative
range of English dishes which well done should be a source
of national pride. Also the reader will find a number of traditional English dishes which threaten to be lost to posterity
since as far as I have been able to discover they have never
been printed and published. Most of these are family recipes
and have been handed down from generation to generation.
The bardic method by which the poems of Homer were pre-
served does exist among cooks but it is unreliable, and in these
days of what are revoltingly described as 'convenience foods'
it is dwindling.

Recipes long forgotten are being revived and English food
is becoming fashionable. Let us hope that home cooking will
keep pace with the trend of fashion. If English food is presented in its true form it will once more take its place as one of
the best cuisines in the world.

Notes

~~~~~~

WEIGHTS AND MEASURES

Wherever possible, I have given the amounts in pints, pounds and ounces to serve four to six people. Occasionally, a cup has been used as a measure and by this I mean a teacup, but since Great Britain is soon to change to the metric system, here is an *approximate* table of dry weights and measures.

$$1 \text{ kilogram} = 1{,}000 \text{ grams} = 2 \text{ lb. } 3 \text{ oz.}$$
$$1 \text{ lb.} = 16 \text{ oz.} = 450 \text{ grams}$$
$$1 \text{ oz.} = 30 \text{ grams}$$

grams	*oz.*		*grams*	*lb./oz.*
15	= $\frac{1}{2}$		225	= 8 ($\frac{1}{2}$ lb.)
30	= 1	($\frac{1}{4}$ kilo)	250	= 9
50	= $1\frac{2}{3}$		450	= 16 (1 lb.)
60	= 2	($\frac{1}{2}$ kilo)	500	= 18
90	= 3		675	= 1 lb. 8 oz.
100	= $3\frac{1}{2}$	($\frac{3}{4}$ kilo)	750	= 1 lb. 10 oz.
113	= 4		900	= 2 lb.
125	= $4\frac{1}{3}$		1 kilo	= 2 lb. 3 oz.
150	= $5\frac{1}{3}$		$1\frac{1}{2}$ kilos	= 3 lb. 5 oz.
170	= 6		2 kilos	= 4 lb. 6 oz.
200	= 7			

Approximate equivalents in volume of the most frequently used ingredients:

Sugar	1 lb. or 450 grams	= 2 cups
	2 oz. or 60 grams	= $\frac{1}{4}$ cup

9

Flour	1 lb. or 450 grams	= 4 cups
(sifted)	2 oz. or 60 grams	= $\frac{1}{2}$ cup
	100 grams	= $\frac{3}{4}$ cup
Butter	1 lb. or 450 grams	= 2 cups
	2 oz. or 60 grams	= $\frac{1}{4}$ cup
	100 grams	= $\frac{1}{3}$ cup less 1 tablespoon

The English tablespoon is equal to 4 teaspoons. (The U.S. standard measuring tablespoon equals 3 teaspoons.)

OVEN HEATS

Oven temperatures for gas and electricity are not given with the recipes in this book since gas and electricity are not universal and it is assumed that indications such as slow, moderate, hot, etc., are enough for any cook using the following recipes. However, for those who wish to check their oven heat an approximate conversion table is given below.

	ELECTRICITY		GAS
	Fahrenheit	*Centigrade*	
very slow	240–275°	116–135°	$\frac{1}{2}$–2
slow	275–325°	135–163°	2–3
moderate	325–375°	163–190°	3–4
moderately hot	375–425°	190–218°	5–6
hot	425–475°	218–246°	7–8
very hot	475–500°	246–260°	9 and over

1. Herbs and Spices

Gervase Markham gave good advice in *The English Huswife 1615* in saying the first step to practising the art of cooking was 'to have knowledge of all sorts of herbs belonging unto the kitchen whether they be for the pot, for sallets, for sauces, for servings or for any other seasoning or adorning, which skill or knowledge of herbs she must get of her own true labour and experience'.

Writing in 1557, Tusser, an East Anglian farmer, lists well over thirty herbs he considered necessary for the kitchen garden, and Gerard's famous Herball first published in 1597 was written primarily for 'gentlewomen'. The Elizabethans ate well and cooking was then an art, herbs and spices playing a big part in the kitchens of that time mainly for preserving food and, I fear, to cover the taste of tainted meat.

In the eighteenth and nineteenth centuries every country house, cottage or farm had a herb garden in constant use close to the kitchen door, but today, mint and parsley seem to be the only herbs in constant use in the English kitchen although herb farms are beginning to flourish and discerning and interested cooks are once more beginning to keep a variety of herbs in their kitchens and gardens.

The indiscriminate use of pungent herbs should be avoided. A good soup becomes a delicious one by the light and subtle sprinkling of a few herbs, but it should not be possible to taste them. A heavy hand with herbs will ruin many a good dish and it is well to keep in mind that dried herbs have a stronger flavour than fresh ones.

A faggot of herbs consists of a sprig of thyme, or marjoram, a stalk or two of parsley, and a bay leaf firmly tied together so that it may be lifted out of the pot before serving.

Bay
Bay leaves are used for flavouring milk, soups and stews or in a faggot of herbs. They have a rather strong flavour and should be used discreetly. The bay tree is usually grown as an ornamental tree in England and it is widely believed that a flourishing bay tree brings health and prosperity to the house.

Caper
Capers grow wild on the rocky coasts of the southern Mediterranean. Picked and pickled in vinegar, they are used as a garnish for boiled fish and crawfish. In England they are mainly used for caper sauce, but they also make an unusual and interesting addition to mayonnaise or a cabbage salad.

Chamomile
Chamomile grows a flower rather like a daisy but with a very characteristic smell and is used mainly for making a tea which soothes the stomach and induces sleep.

Chervil
Chervil has a mild flavour of aniseed and is used in soups and stews or in a mixed salad.

Chives
Chives taste mildly of onions and are particularly good for seasoning omelettes, scrambled eggs, salad and cottage cheese. They also provide a good garnish for boiled potatoes and other vegetables.

Cloves
Cloves are the dried flower buds of the clove tree. They have a spicy aromatic flavour and are used in sauces and meat dishes and in fruit puddings and pies, particularly with apple.

Dill
The dried seeds and fresh leaves are widely used on the continent, but it is mainly known in England for its pharmaceutical use in dill water for settling babies' stomachs. The feathery leaves may be used instead of fennel, the flavour of which it closely resembles. It prefers a dry soil and grows well in a sunny corner of the garden.

Fennel
Fennel has a feathery leaf and a mild flavour of aniseed which is good for soups and fish while the stalks may be used raw in salads or cooked like celery.

Garlic
At one time widely used in English cookery, garlic is now coming back into favour from the continent. Use with discretion in soups, salads, stews, etc.

Mace
Mace is the dried outer covering of the nutmeg and has a milder flavour than nutmeg. It is used for flavouring fish, sauces, stuffings, etc.

Marjoram
Fresh pot marjoram (*Origanum onites*) and sweet marjoram (*Origanum majorana*) are both useful in soups, sauces and some egg dishes. Dried marjoram is more pungent than fresh and should be used sparingly.

Mint
Spearmint is the most commonly used variety but apple mint and other flavours make a welcome change. Mint tea makes a delicious digestive drink. Mint sauce is usually made from spearmint.

Nutmeg
Grown in the East Indies, nutmeg is widely used for flavouring custards, puddings, preserves, etc. Grated nutmeg has a stronger flavour than mace which is the outer skin of the nutmeg.

Parsley
A biennial, parsley is used as a seasoning or as a garnish. It is one of the best sources of the vitamins A and C and possesses a high content of other minerals. Having a mild flavour, it is one of the few herbs which warrants a generous hand.

Pepper
Black and white pepper come from the same berry. Black pepper being the whole fruit which becomes white pepper after the hull has been removed. Ground black pepper is stronger and has more flavour than white. Widely used in hot climates, pepper stimulates perspiration and acts as a cooling agent. The berries are known as peppercorns and are used in pickling. Freshly ground in a pepper-mill, they give a more definite flavour to a dish.

There are several varieties of red pepper; cayenne is the one most commonly used in English cookery to flavour cheese and other savoury dishes.

Rosemary
A sprig or two of rosemary tucked into a roast of lamb or veal imparts a delicious flavour to the meat but should be removed before serving.

Sage
Sage is mainly used for stuffing but is also good in soups, or strewn lightly over pork chops. Sage tea was brewed in England before China or Indian tea was known, and was used as a stomach settler rather than a stimulant.

Summer Savory
A hardy annual aromatic plant useful for soups, stews, meat, and tomato salad, summer savory is very similar in flavour to the Italian origano or the Greek rigani (*Origanum Pulchrum*) for which it is a good substitute.

Sweet Basil
Mainly used as a seasoning for soups, stews and sauces, it makes a pretty potted plant. It may also be used in tomato or cucumber salads.

Tarragon
Used for flavouring poultry, vinegar, dressings, sauces, etc., it is more widely used in France than in England.

Thyme
There are two varieties of thyme, common thyme and lemon thyme. Both are used for seasoning savouries and soups. Lemon thyme is less pungent than common thyme and is used mainly for forcemeats.

2. Sauces and Dressings

A sauce, sweet or savoury, hot or cold, adds interest and variety to a number of dishes though English cooking in the main does not call for as wide a range of sauces as that of other countries. Nevertheless, a good sauce-maker implies a good cook. Anyone who takes trouble with sauces shows an appreciation and understanding of food and is unlikely to spoil its preparation. Making gravy out of a packet is a habit to be deplored when good gravy is so simply made by scraping round the roasting tin in which the meat has been cooked after the surplus fat has been poured off, adding salt and pepper and a little hot stock, wine or vegetable water.

A foundation white sauce, carefully made and with the addition of flavourings, sweet and savoury, will improve many a dish, but it is most important that it be well made and not just flavoured milk thickened with cornflour.

Plain flour is a successful thickening agent for most sauces, although arrowroot and cornflour are sometimes more suitable, as for instance when eggs are used and the sauce must not boil for fear of curdling the eggs. It is advisable, however, to let a sauce boil for a minute or two once flour has been added in order to break down the starch or the sauce will not be successful and will carry the disagreeable taste of flour and water paste. Such sauces must also be stirred constantly or they will become lumpy. Experience tells a cook the quantities required and those given should be regarded as a guide only. A knob of butter stirred in at the last moment is the secret of

16

most white sauces and the addition of wine, rum or brandy to
a sauce should take place a few minutes before serving.

Apple Sauce

4 *large cooking apples*	4–6 *cloves*
3 *tablespoons sugar*	1 *oz. butter*
juice of ½ lemon	*water*

Choose apples which fall when baked, that is to say apples such
as Bramleys which will mash easily. Peel, core and slice the
apples. Put them into a saucepan with the sugar, lemon juice,
cloves and enough water to prevent them from burning. Stew
them gently until soft enough to beat to a pulp. Remove
cloves. Stir in the butter and beat until smooth with a wooden
spoon. Pour into a sauceboat and serve hot.

If preferred, the apples may be cooked in an earthenware
dish in the oven and sent to table in the same dish, in which
case they are not beaten.

Serve with roast pork and roast duckling.

Apricot Sauce

12 *apricots*	*sugar to taste*
water	*salt*
1 *glass sherry*	

Cut the apricots in half and remove the stones, a few of which
may be cracked and the kernels added to the sauce. Put the
fruit into a saucepan with a little water according to the juici-
ness of the fruit. Add sugar to taste and a pinch of salt. Stew
until the fruit is soft enough to put through a coarse sieve or use
an electric blender to reduce the apricots to a purée. Return
the fruit to the saucepan, add the sherry and reheat, but do not
allow the sauce to boil after the addition of the sherry.

If fresh fruit is not available, dried apricots may be used, in which case they should be soaked overnight. Apricot sauce is very good served with canary pudding.

Black Butter Sauce

Of course, this sauce is not really black for if it were it would be burnt and inedible.

2 oz. butter	lemon juice
½ teaspoon wine vinegar or	1 teaspoon chopped parsley

Melt the butter in a pan and watch it like a hawk until it is golden-brown and foaming. Remove from the heat and add the wine vinegar or lemon juice and a teaspoon of finely chopped parsley. Return to the heat, cook for just one minute and serve at once. Serve with poached brains or grilled fish.

Brandy Butter

4 oz. butter	1 wineglass brandy
6 oz. caster sugar	salt

Soften the butter to a cream but do not let it melt. Sieve the sugar and beat it into the butter little by little, adding the brandy drop by drop until both have been absorbed by the butter and it becomes light and fluffy. Work in a good pinch of salt, if unsalted butter is used, and pile it into a glass dish to serve. Keep in a cold place until required. Serve with Christmas pudding as an alternative to rum sauce.

Brandy Sauce

1 pint milk	2 eggs
3 tablespoons sugar	2 tablespoons brandy
salt	

Warm the milk with three tablespoons of sugar and a pinch

of salt. Beat two eggs very well and add them to the milk. Stir constantly until the sauce thickens just before boiling point. Remove from the fire and add two tablespoons of brandy. This method requires care or the sauce may curdle or become lumpy. A surer way is to use a double boiler or a basin over a pan of simmering hot water which must not be allowed to bubble and boil too vigorously. In this case, beat the eggs well with the sugar, then add the milk and a pinch of salt and beat again. Pour into the top of the double boiler or into a basin if used and stir from time to time until the sauce thickens. Remove from the fire and add the brandy just before serving. Good with chocolate pudding.

Bread Sauce

½ *small stale loaf*	¾ *pint milk*
1 *small onion*	½ *oz. butter*
6 *cloves*	*salt, pepper*

Remove the crusts from the bread and crumb it finely. Stick the cloves into the onion and put it into the milk to infuse while the breadcrumbs are being prepared. Add the breadcrumbs to the milk with the butter and season to taste. Leave to simmer very gently for at least twenty minutes, stirring from time to time as bread sauce can easily burn or turn into a poultice. Remove the onion and cloves before serving. If preferred, a blade of mace or grated nutmeg may be used instead of cloves for flavouring and the addition of a tablespoon of cream enriches the sauce enormously.

Caper Sauce (1)

½ *pint white sauce (p.* 32)	1 *teaspoon chopped parsley*
1 *tablespoon capers*	1 *teaspoon tarragon vinegar*

Make half a pint of white sauce and add the capers, chopped

if you like, a teaspoon of finely chopped parsley and a teaspoon of tarragon vinegar. Serve with fish, boiled beef or calf's head.

Caper Sauce (2) (for Brains)

3 oz. butter
1 tablespoon wine vinegar
2 tablespoons capers
salt and freshly ground pepper

Melt the butter in a frying pan and when it is just turning brown and foamy add the vinegar and the capers. Swill round in the pan and pour over the brains. Cover the casserole and re-heat in the oven.

Cheese Sauce

To make a rich cheese sauce add four ounces of matured Cheddar, or three ounces of Cheddar and one ounce of Parmesan, to one pint of white sauce. Stir continually until the cheese has melted and the sauce is smooth and glossy. It should be used at once but if it has to stand a few scraps of butter melted on top of the sauce will help to prevent a skin forming, but it must be kept warm. This applies to any white sauce.

Chelford Sauce

1 tablespoon butter
1 medium-size onion
2 teaspoons vinegar
1 teaspoon lemon juice
1 teaspoon Worcestershire sauce
1 tablespoon soft brown sugar
2 tablespoons tomato paste
$\frac{1}{2}$ teaspoon mustard
$1\frac{1}{2}$ teacups boiling water
salt and pepper

Melt the butter in a saucepan. Add the finely chopped onion and one teacup of boiling water and cook until the onion is soft and transparent. Mix all the other ingredients together with the rest of the boiling water and stir into the pan. Simmer the sauce for twenty minutes and serve with boiled tongue, calf's head or baked ham.

Cranberry Sauce

$\frac{1}{2}$ *lb. cranberries*   *2 tablespoons sugar*
1 *lemon* $\frac{1}{2}$ *oz. butter*

Put the cranberries in a pan with just enough water to prevent them from burning. Add a sliver of lemon peel and the sugar and let them cook very slowly with the pan lid on for twenty minutes to half an hour when the fruit should be pulpy. Remove from the fire, beat in the butter and squeeze in the lemon juice. If the sauce is required to be clear, rub the fruit through a sieve before adding the butter and lemon juice.

Cucumber Sauce

For serving with poached salmon or salmon trout, this sauce is delicious if a little rich and a change from the usual accompaniments to these delectable fish.

Make a good white sauce and add as much chopped and peeled fresh cucumber as the sauce will take. Season to taste and, if liked, stir in a tablespoon of dry white wine just before serving. Care must be taken to add the wine slowly and when the sauce is off the heat as the wine might curdle the sauce.

Send to table in a warmed sauceboat.

Cumberland Sauce

Named after the Duke of Cumberland, King of Hanover, this delicious sauce goes well with all kinds of cold meats and also with ox tongue served hot. It is perhaps more popular in

Germany today than in England where it is said to have originated.

1 *tablespoon chopped shallot*	*juice of* ½ *orange*
½ *tablespoon shredded orange peel*	1 *teaspoon mustard*
	generous pinch of salt, pepper, cayenne and ground ginger
½ *tablespoon shredded lemon peel*	1 *teacup red currant jelly*
juice of ½ *lemon*	1 *teacup port or red wine*

Blanch the chopped shallot in boiling water, drain it dry and mix it with the shredded peel and juice of the orange and lemon to the already melted red currant jelly. Add the mustard and seasoning to taste and lastly the port or red wine. Stir well but do not strain.

Curry Sauce

1 *oz. butter*	½ *pint milk*
1 *tablespoon flour*	1 *bay leaf*
½ *teaspoon curry powder or paste*	*salt and pepper*

Melt the butter in a saucepan, add the flour and half a teaspoon of curry powder or paste; more if you like it hot. Stir over a low heat for two minutes, add half a pint of milk scalded with a bay leaf and season with salt and a little pepper. Let the sauce simmer gently for ten minutes. Serve with lobster and rice (p. 74).

Custard Sauce

1 *pint milk*	2 *eggs*
1 *pod vanilla*	3 *oz. sugar*

Put a pod of vanilla into the milk and warm to blood heat. Beat together two eggs with three ounces of sugar and add the warmed milk. Pour into a bowl and place over a saucepan of very hot water or use a double saucepan. The water should be kept just simmering, not boiling, or the custard may scramble. Keep stirring until the sauce thickens when it is ready for use. The addition of cream, a pinch of salt and a tablespoon of brandy enriches this sauce.

Dr. Kitchiner's Sauce

'Chop some parsley leaves very fine, quarter two or three pickled cucumbers (I think this means gherkins) or walnuts, divide them into small squares and set them by ready; put into a saucepan a bit of butter the size of an egg; when it is melted, stir in a tablespoon of fine flour and about half a pint of the broth in which the beef has been boiled; add a tablespoon of vinegar, the like quantity of mushroom catsup, or port wine, or both, and a teaspoon of prepared mustard; let it simmer together till it is as thick as you wish, put in the parsley and pickles to get warm, and pour it over the beef, or rather send it up in a sauce-tureen.' (*Cook's Oracle*, 1823)

Dr. Kitchiner's recipe for Bubble and Squeak is for using brined boiled beef which is why the sauce he invented to go with it allows half a pint of broth. Any meat stock seasoned with salt and pepper will serve as a substitute if the beef used is not boiled.

Egg Sauce

3 *or* 4 *eggs*   ½ *pint white sauce* (*p.* 32)

Put three or four eggs into cold water and bring them to the boil. Let them boil for ten minutes then plunge them into cold water. When cool enough to handle, strip off the shells and chop them not too fine. Prepare half a pint of rich white sauce and add the chopped eggs at boiling point. Stir gently

over the fire for one minute and serve very hot. Serve with
poached or steamed fish or with fish cakes.

Hollandaise Sauce

A rich sauce which requires constant attention when making.
Although Dutch in origin, it has become widely used in both
the French and English kitchen.

4 *egg yolks*	4 *oz. butter*
2 *tablespoons warm water*	1 *tablespoon lemon juice*

Beat the egg yolks with the warm water and place over a pan
of hot water. Heat very slowly beating briskly until light and
foamy. Add the butter a little at a time beating continuously
until it is all absorbed. Season lightly and stir in the lemon
juice. On no account add the butter too quickly or the sauce
will curdle. Hollandaise sauce is served with fish or vegetables.

Horseradish Sauce

Although bottled horseradish is mostly used these days, it is
so much better freshly made if horseradish root is available
and, apart from a temporary discomfort to the eyes, it is
simply and quickly prepared.

4 *tablespoons grated horse-*	$\frac{1}{2}$ *teaspoon pepper*
radish	2 *teaspoons made mustard*
1 *teaspoon sugar*	1 *tablespoon vinegar*
1 *teaspoon salt*	4 *tablespoons double cream*

Grate the horseradish as finely as possible and mix it well with
the sugar, salt, pepper and mustard. Add the vinegar and
lastly the cream. The sauce should have the consistency of
thick cream. It is served traditionally with roast beef and often
with smoked trout.

Another method is to grate the horseradish finely and simply mix it with a little thick fresh cream. This is a much blander sauce and not so sharp to the palate.

Lobster Sauce

Follow the recipe for shrimp sauce (p. 30) using the lobster meat from the legs and any untidy bits left over from dressing a boiled lobster. If the lobster is a hen then add the coral to the sauce as well.

Francatelli used lobster meat cut into small pieces as well as the juice of half a lemon, a teaspoon of anchovy and a pinch of cayenne pepper, but the price of lobsters today prohibits most people from doing this.

Marinade

The word marinade (or marinate) comes from an old Spanish word meaning 'to pickle'. It is the acid of the marinade that does the work of softening the tough fibres in meat and the marinade itself adds a subtle flavour to ordinary foods and lifts them out of the commonplace. The recipe given is for a light marinade and if a stronger one is called for, sweet basil, marjoram, rosemary, tarragon or any herb the cook fancies may be added, but with discretion.

1 *small lemon*	2 *small bay leaves*
1 *small raw carrot*	2 *cloves*
3 *tablespoons wine vinegar*	3 *sprigs parsley*
1 *tablespoon olive oil*	8 *peppercorns*
1 *sprig thyme*	*salt*

Slice the lemon and carrot as thinly as possible and put them in a shallow earthenware dish with the olive oil, vinegar and crushed herbs. Season with salt and place the meat, fish or game in the dish. Leave to marinate in a cool place for several hours, overnight if possible, turning from time to time.

Marmalade Sauce

2 teaspoons marmalade   1 teaspoon cornflour
1 teaspoon caster sugar   juice of $\frac{1}{2}$ a lemon
$\frac{1}{2}$ pint water   salt

Put the marmalade, sugar, salt and water into a saucepan and bring to the boil. Add the cornflour, mixed with a little cold water, and boil until the sauce is clear. This should take about five minutes. Stir in the lemon juice and serve hot.

Mayonnaise

$\frac{1}{2}$ teaspoon sugar $\frac{1}{2}$ pint olive oil
salt and pepper   1 tablespoon lemon juice or
1 egg yolk   wine vinegar

Put the sugar, salt and pepper into a bowl, mix together, then drop in the egg yolk and stir with a wooden spoon. Remember that a good mayonnaise is only achieved by slow steady stirring. Stir strongly for a minute or so then drip in one tablespoon of olive oil very slowly until it is absorbed. Continue to drip in the rest of the olive oil steadily, with the lemon juice or vinegar, until the desired consistency and flavour is reached. Should the mayonnaise curdle, start again with a clean bowl and another egg yolk and gradually work in the curdled mayonnaise.

A few chopped chives, capers, or two chopped anchovy fillets with their oil and a dust of paprika stirred in at the last minute make an interesting change when serving with cold crab, lobster, salmon or crawfish.

Mint Sauce

2 *tablespoons chopped mint*   4 *tablespoons malt* or *wine*
1 *tablespoon sugar*   *vinegar*

Remove the leaves from the stalks of the mint and chop them
as finely as possible. This is made easier by chopping some of
the sugar with the mint. Add the rest of the sugar and stir in
the vinegar until the sugar is dissolved. Mint sauce should be
made at least two hours before required so that the vinegar
becomes impregnated with the flavour of the mint. More
vinegar may be added if liked; it is a matter of taste. Mint
sauce is usually served with roast lamb.

Mint Sauce, Bottled

6 *tablespoons chopped mint* $\frac{1}{4}$ *pint malt vinegar*
4 *oz. sugar*

Strip the leaves from the stalks and chop them finely. Put them
into a basin and cover them with sugar. Bring the vinegar to
the boil and pour over the mint and stir until the sugar is quite
dissolved. Pour into a jar and cork down when cold.

Mushroom Sauce

8 *oz. mushrooms* $\frac{1}{2}$ *pint milk*
2 *oz. butter*   2 *tablespoons flour*
salt, pepper   *thick cream*

Wipe and slice the mushrooms and put them into a heavy-
bottomed saucepan in which the butter has been melted.
They will run a little juice and should simmer gently until
soft. Add the milk leaving a little to mix with the flour for
thickening the sauce. Season and just before serving add some
thick cream.

Mustard Sauce

2 oz. flour	1 teaspoon malt vinegar
2 oz. butter	1 teaspoon tarragon vinegar
1 tablespoon dry mustard	1 teaspoon sugar
½ pint stock	salt

Melt the butter and stir in the flour and mustard vigorously.
Add the warmed stock gradually, beating all the time. Lastly,
add the vinegar, sugar and salt and beat over the fire to a
creamy consistency. Serve with grilled herrings.

Onion Sauce

1 lb. onions	½ pint milk
butter	salt and pepper
1 dessertspoon flour	nutmeg

This is an old-fashioned sauce and a very good one to serve
with roast lamb. Peel and cut up one pound of onions. Put
them into a heavy-bottomed saucepan and barely cover with
cold water. This removes the bite from the onions and ensures
a gentle sauce. When the onions are cooked they may be
chopped roughly or put through a coarse sieve. Return them
to the pan with a good knob of butter and stir in the sieved
flour and half a pint of warmed milk. Season with salt, pepper
and a grate or two of nutmeg and bring to the boil. Cook for
ten minutes and serve very hot.

Orange Sauce

2 Seville oranges	gravy
1 glass sherry	salt and pepper

Squeeze the oranges and keep the juice on one side. Remove
the pith. Put the orange peel into a saucepan with a little

water and boil until soft, then drain and cut into thin strips. Add the peel, with the orange juice and sherry, to the gravy made from the juices run from the roast duck. If the sauce is not sour enough, add a little lemon juice, and if not sweet enough, add a little sugar, but remember that a true orange sauce is an acid sauce.

Parsley Sauce

1 *pint white sauce (p. 32)*   3 *tablespoons chopped parsley*
                                butter

Make a rich white sauce and add the finely chopped parsley, discarding the stems unless a green sauce is required. Stir in an extra knob of butter and see that the sauce does not boil after the parsley has been added. Serve with poached or baked fish, ox tongue and ham.

Rum Sauce

2 *oz. butter*   1 *oz. sugar*
1 *oz. flour*   2 *tablespoons rum*
1 *pint milk*   *salt*

Melt the butter in a saucepan, add the sieved flour and beat over a low fire to a smooth paste. Add the warmed milk, the sugar and a pinch of salt, stirring constantly to keep the sauce smooth. Stir in the rum just before serving and add an extra lump of butter to ensure a bland sauce. Serve with Christmas pudding as an alternative to brandy butter.

Salad Dressings

Oil and Vinegar

Wine vinegar, never malt vinegar, is a rule for a successful salad dressing. Sugar is not necessary if a good wine vinegar is used and even this can be improved by adding a tablespoon or two of burgundy or claret to your bottle of wine vinegar.

A good pinch of salt, a generous grind of pepper mixed with one tablespoon red wine vinegar and two tablespoons olive oil in the salad bowl at table is the ideal way to dress a salad. However, these days when time counts and salads are frequently served with every main meal it is useful to make enough dressing at one time to last for several meals.

Put one-third wine vinegar to two-thirds olive oil in a screw-top jar. Add salt and freshly ground black pepper to taste. Shake it well until the oil and vinegar emulsify then pour a little over the salad.

Cream

For those who prefer a cream to an oil and vinegar dressing for their salads, here is Meg Dod's receipt for 'Salad Sauce' (1862):

'Rub the yolks of two hard-boiled eggs very smooth with a little rich cream. When well mixed, add a teaspoonful of made mustard and a little salt, a spoonful of olive oil, and when this is mixed smooth, put in as much plain eschalot, cucumber, tarragon or chili vinegar as will give the proper acidity to the sauce—about two large spoonfuls; add a little pounded sugar if the flavour is liked. Salad sauce may be rendered more pungent by the addition of cayenne, minced onion or eschalot, or more herb-flavoured vinegar. Put the smooth sauce in a dish and either lay the cut herbs lightly over it, or mix them well with it.'

Shrimp Sauce

1 *gill picked shrimps*	*salt, cayenne, nutmeg*
1 *teaspoon anchovy essence*	*butter*
1 *pint white sauce (p. 32)*	

Add a gill of boiled and picked shrimps and one teaspoon anchovy essence to one pint white sauce. Season to taste with salt, cayenne pepper and a grate of nutmeg. Simmer for ten minutes and stir in a knob of butter just before serving. Serve with baked or poached fish or with fish cakes.

Tomato Sauce

If using fresh tomatoes they must be very ripe indeed or the sauce will be pale and unappetizing. When fresh ripe tomatoes are not available, tinned whole tomatoes, preferably the long variety, may be used instead. A dessertspoon of tomato purée adds flavour and deepens the colour.

2 *lb. ripe tomatoes*	1 *bay leaf*
2 *oz. butter*	1 *sprig sweet basil*
2 *heaped tablespoons grated onion*	1 *wineglass red wine*
1 *level dessertspoon sugar*	$\frac{1}{2}$ *pint water*
$\frac{1}{2}$ *teaspoon powdered cinnamon* or 1 *stick cinnamon*	*salt and pepper*

Skin the tomatoes and put them through a coarse sieve to reduce them to pulp and remove the seeds. The skin will come away easily if the tomatoes are steeped in boiling water for one minute. Put the grated onions into a heavy saucepan, barely cover them with water, and let them simmer for five minutes, by which time the water should nearly have disappeared. This takes the strong odour out of the onions but is not necessary if Spanish onions are used. Add the butter, tomatoes, herbs, sugar and seasoning and simmer gently over a low flame for three quarters of an hour, adding a little water if necessary. Five minutes before serving remove the bay leaf and stick of cinnamon if used and pour in the wine.

White Sauce

This is a basic sauce to which may be added flavourings both salt and sweet.

3 *oz. butter*	1 *pint milk*
2 *tablespoons flour*	*salt*

Melt the butter in a heavy saucepan and with a wooden spoon stir in the sieved flour and salt. When the mixture begins to leave the sides of the pan, add the warmed milk little by little, beating vigorously all the time to keep the sauce smooth and glossy and free from lumps. Let it bubble a little before adding other ingredients.

Sauce for Wild Duck

1 *saltspoon salt*	1 *dessertspoon Worcester*
½ *saltspoon cayenne*	*sauce*
1 *dessertspoon lemon juice*	3 *dessertspoons port wine*
1 *dessertspoon sugar*	

Mix well together, heat and pour over the bird, *or*

1 *good teaspoon black*	1 *tablespoon Worcester sauce*
pepper	1 *teaspoon mushroom ketchup*
1 *dessertspoon fine sugar*	3 *tablespoons port wine*
1 *tablespoon lemon juice*	

Mix together and make very hot and add a knob of butter the size of a nutmeg.

Wine Sauce for Sweet Puddings

This is Eliza Acton's recipe for wine sauce but I have taken the liberty of substituting cornflour in place of plain flour as it makes the sauce more appetizing.

rind of ½ a lemon
wineglass of water
2 oz. brown sugar
1 oz. butter

2 level teaspoons cornflour
wineglass of sherry, madeira
or sweet white wine

Cut very thinly the rind of half a large lemon and put into a saucepan with the water and brown sugar. Simmer gently for ten to fifteen minutes. Take out the lemon peel and stir into the sauce one ounce of butter into which two level teaspoons of cornflour have been smoothly kneaded. Add the wine and, when quite hot, serve the sauce without delay.

Port wine sauce may be made the same way using a wineglass of port and adding a dessertspoon of lemon juice or the zest and juice of half a large orange. Add a little freshly grated nutmeg and a little more sugar if required.

3. Stuffings

Banana Stuffing

As used for stuffing grouse or partridge at Boodles Club in London. Peel and cut up some ripe bananas. Mash them well with a silver fork and mix with up to one level teaspoon of freshly ground black pepper, one of salt and a little lemon juice.

Chestnut Stuffing

2 *lb. chestnuts* *milk*
2 *oz. breadcrumbs* 1 *dessertspoon sugar*
2 *oz. butter* *salt and pepper*
1 *turkey liver*

Make a slit in the top of each chestnut and boil them for half an hour by which time they should be cooked. Remove the skins as soon as they are cool enough to handle. Rub them through a coarse sieve or pound them and mix together with the breadcrumbs, melted butter, turkey liver, a little milk, sugar and seasoning. Mix well and use for stuffing a turkey.

A good stuffing is also made from equal quantities of sausage meat and boiled and chopped chestnuts, in which case the breadcrumbs are omitted.

Crayfish Stuffing

This is an unusual and rather rare stuffing taken from an old family recipe used in the days when crayfish were more easily obtainable than they are today. It was used to stuff a turkey.

For a twelve-pound bird

turkey liver	1 tablespoon chopped parsley
4 oz. calves' liver	½ teaspoon allspice
3 crayfish tails	sweet herbs
2 rashers bacon	salt and pepper

Mince the turkey and calves' liver and add the pounded cray-fish tails, the finely chopped bacon, chopped parsley, allspice, a small bunch of sweet herbs, salt and pepper. Stuff the bird and roast in the usual manner.

Forcemeat Stuffing

4 oz. breadcrumbs	1 lemon
3 oz. chopped suet	pepper and salt
1 tablespoon chopped parsley	1 egg
1 teaspoon lemon thyme	milk

Put the breadcrumbs into a bowl with the suet, herbs, lemon juice and grated rind of the lemon. Season with salt and pepper and bind with the well-beaten egg. If the stuffing is too dry, moisten with a little milk. Use for meat, chicken or fish.

Goose Stuffing (1)

goose liver	1 small bay leaf
½ lb. prunes	1 lemon
¾ lb. rice	1 egg
6 shallots	salt and pepper
2 oz. butter	

Blanch the liver in boiling water for a few minutes then chop it finely and keep on one side. The prunes should be soaked overnight or stewed lightly in order to remove the stones easily; they should be chopped coarsely. Cook the rice in salted water until nearly done then drain it well and put into a mixing bowl. Crush the bayleaf in the hand and add to the rice with the liver, chopped shallots and prunes, melted butter, the grated lemon peel and juice of half or the whole lemon if small. Season with salt and pepper and bind together with the beaten egg. The stuffing is now ready for use but the flavour is much improved if it is left in a covered bowl overnight.

Goose Stuffing (2)

4 oz. breadcrumbs
2 oz. grated suet
grated peel of 1 lemon
lemon juice
1 teaspoon dried sage

1 crushed clove of garlic
1 egg
1 teacup milk
salt and pepper to taste

Mix the breadcrumbs with the suet, add the grated lemon peel, the sage, a squeeze of lemon juice and the garlic and bind with the egg beaten in the milk. Season well with salt and freshly ground black pepper. The stuffing is improved if pounded with a pestle and mortar and is particularly good if the goose is boned and served cold.

Mashed Potato Stuffing

2 lb. potatoes
1 oz. butter
1 tablespoon milk

1 onion
salt and pepper

Peel the potatoes, cover with cold salted water and boil rapidly until cooked. Drain them well and shake over a flame or in the fresh air to dry out. Mash and blend in the butter, milk, and a finely chopped or grated onion. Season with salt and pepper and use to stuff a goose.

Sage and Onion Stuffing

2 *large onions*	2 *teaspoons chopped sage* or
2 *oz. breadcrumbs*	1 *teaspoon dried sage*
3 *oz. butter*	*salt and pepper*

Peel the onions, chop them coarsely and put them into a heavy-bottomed pan. Barely cover with water and cook until the onions are soft, then add the breadcrumbs, butter, chopped sage and season well with salt and pepper. If using dried sage (less will be required as dried herbs are always stronger) rub it between your hands to bring out the flavour.

Add a little hot water if the stuffing seems dry. Put the stuffing into a greased earthenware oven dish, dot with butter and cook in a hot oven about one hour, or use to stuff a turkey, duck, pork or breast of lamb.

Sausage Forcemeat

1½ *lb. sausage meat, veal* or	1 *or 2 grated onions*
pork freshly minced	3 *oz. minced fat bacon*
3 *oz. white breadcrumbs*	1 *beaten egg*
1 *dessertspoon chopped mixed*	*stock to moisten*
herbs	*salt and pepper*

Mix all the ingredients well together, using the egg and a little stock if necessary to moisten the stuffing. Season well and use for stuffing a turkey or goose.

Sausage Meat Stuffing

2 *lb. sausage meat*	*mixed herbs*
1 *onion*	1 *glass sherry*

37

Sausage meat as bought from most butchers tends to be rather flavourless; mix some finely chopped onion, a few mixed herbs and a glass of sherry with it before stuffing a turkey or capon. Some cooks like to add boiled chestnuts, roughly chopped, to this stuffing.

Veal Stuffing

3 oz. lean bacon	1 teaspoon sweet marjoram
4 oz. shredded suet	4 oz. breadcrumbs
1 small lemon	1 egg
2 teaspoons chopped parsley	salt and pepper
1 teaspoon thyme	

Mince the bacon finely and mix with the suet, the grated lemon peel, the chopped or dried herbs and the breadcrumbs. Season with salt and pepper and bind with the well-beaten egg. The stuffing should be light but firm. It may also be used for stuffing poultry. The mixture may also be made into balls and fried until golden in cooking oil and can be served with hare or rabbit.

4. Cheese and Savoury Dishes

CHEESE

In days gone by, cheese-making was dependent on a number of factors. The quality of the milk, the pasture the cattle fed on and the time of year all determined the quality and type of cheese. Dale or Moorland cheeses were only made in the spring, cattle grazing by the sands of the Dee produced rich milk for some of the best Cheshire cheeses and many Welsh cheeses were only made in the month of May, while others were made in September.

Today, many local cheeses are no longer made at all and a considerable number of the well-known ones are produced in factories. Cheeses originally made in the places whose names they bear have unfortunately become names for a type of cheese and are often made far from their place of origin. We even have Canadian Cheddar.

In the case of hard cheeses, the bacteria is artificially cultivated and added to the milk, while in the case of Stilton, one of England's most famous cheeses, some of which is now made in Somerset, a mould culture, *Penicillium Roqueforti*, is added when production begins in a new area, after which the buildings become so permeated with the culture it is no longer necessary to add it artificially.

The first Stilton was made in the early part of the eighteenth century at Quenby Hall near Leicester. Elizabeth Scarbrow used to make a famous cheese, known as Lady Beaumont's Cheese, in the dairy there. When she married she took the recipe with her and made it in her own dairy at Little Dalby where it became known as Quenby cheese. Of her two daughters, one married Cooper Thornhill, the landlord of the Bell Inn at Stilton in Huntingdonshire and the other married a farmer named Paulet of Wymondham. The farmer's wife continued to make Quenby cheese and one Christmas she sent one as a present to her brother-in-law at Stilton. The Bell Inn was a stage on the Great North Road and the landlord served the cheese to the passengers by whom it was so much liked that he told his sister-in-law he would take every cheese she could make. It became known as Stilton cheese although it was never made at Stilton. It is, however, I believe, still made at nearby Melton Mowbray.

Nevertheless, despite the wholesale manufacture of what was once a home industry, English country cheeses are returning to favour, encouraged possibly by the fashion for wine and cheese parties. While foreign cheeses have a wide distribution in England today, a good Cheshire, Lancashire or double Gloucester is not too easily come by except in their counties of origin.

Nantwich and Whitchurch produce excellent Cheshire cheeses and Garstang in Lancashire provides some delicious cheeses of varying strengths from mild and crumbly to very strong according to age and maturity. Leigh Toaster, a once-famous cooking cheese, is still obtainable in some shops in the North of England but there are few shops in London and the South where I have been able to find it or indeed find anyone who has even heard of it.

SAVOURIES

English savouries, served as a separate course at the end of the meal, are the origin of many of the dishes in this chapter. They can of course be served equally well as light lunch or supper dishes.

Angels on Horseback

In the days when oysters were of no more esteem than cockles and winkles and came into the same price category, Angels on Horseback were frequently served as an alternative to sweets at the end of a meal. Mrs. Beeton's recipe allows for twelve plump oysters to be used at a total cost of two shillings! Today, the cost would be prohibitive if fresh oysters were to be used but possible now that tinned oysters are obtainable.

12 *oysters*	*herbs*
6 *rashers streaky bacon*	*hot buttered toast*
lemon juice	

Wrap each oyster in half a thin rasher of bacon and secure with a toothpick, or run them on to a thin skewer. Squeeze a little lemon juice over each oyster before rolling it in the bacon. Scatter a few herbs over each one and either grill them or cook in a quick oven for five or six minutes. Serve on hot buttered toast.

Artichokes with Cheese

12 *globe artichokes*	1 *teaspoon chopped parsley*
3 *oz. butter*	1 *teaspoon chopped shallot*
2 *tablespoons grated cheese*	*salt*
½ *glass white wine*	*lemon juice*

Choose large plump young artichokes and allow two per person. Remove the tough outer leaves, slice about one inch off the tops of the inner leaves, cut the stem close and if there is one, remove the choke with a sharp knife. As each artichoke is prepared, rub it over with the cut side of half a lemon and throw quickly into a bowl of water in which you have mixed two tablespoons of flour, a handful of kitchen salt and the juice of a lemon. This is to prevent the artichokes from discolouring which they do very quickly.

Put the artichoke hearts into boiling salted water, add some lemon juice and boil for fifteen minutes when they should be cooked. Remove them from the pan and drain well. Roll the artichokes in melted butter and grated cheese and arrange them in a buttered baking-dish. Pour the wine over the artichokes and place them in a hot oven for about ten minutes when the cheese should have melted. Meanwhile prepare a sauce of melted butter, a finely chopped shallot, some chopped parsley and lemon juice and pour over the artichokes just before serving. Tinned artichokes may be used if fresh unobtainable.

Bacon and Cheese Pie

1 *lb. short pastry (p. 167)*	4 *rashers streaky bacon*
potatoes	2 *eggs*
6 *oz. cheese (Cheddar or similar)*	1 *teacup milk*
	salt and pepper
1 *onion*	

Line a shallow pie dish with thinly rolled short pastry and prick the bottom with a fork. Cover the pastry with finely sliced raw potatoes, a liberal layer of grated or sliced cheese and a layer of finely sliced or grated onion and some chopped streaky bacon. Add one more layer of potatoes. Beat two eggs with one teacup of milk, season with a little salt and pepper, and pour over the contents of the dish. Moisten the edges of the pastry and cover with a thinly rolled layer, pinching the edges together. Make two slits in the top of the pie, brush with a little-beaten egg and milk to give a glaze and place in a hot oven near the top for half an hour to set the pastry, then remove to a lower shelf and reduce the heat to moderate. Bake for about one hour and serve hot. This dish may be prepared beforehand and re-heated.

Bubble and Squeak

Why it is so called I cannot discover, but it is an old English dish dating back to the sixteenth century. Dr. Kitchiner gives a recipe for this dish in the *Cook's Oracle*, published in 1823, but I prefer that given in Warne's *Model Cookery*, also published over a century ago.

1 *lb. cold boiled potatoes*	*butter*
1 *lb. boiled cabbage*	*salt and pepper*
several slices of cold beef	

Chop the cold potatoes and boiled cabbage, season with salt and pepper and fry in butter until brown. Lightly fry the slices of meat, but not too much or they will become hard. Arrange the meat in a hot dish, pile on the cabbage and potato, and serve very hot, with a salad or Dr. Kitchiner's sauce which he invented to go with it (p. 23).

Cauliflower Cheese

1 *large cauliflower*	3 *oz. grated cheese*
1 *pint white sauce* (*p.* 32)	*salt and pepper*

Break a cauliflower head into suitable pieces and barely cover them with boiling salted water. Boil rapidly for not more than ten minutes, then remove from the pan and drain. The cauliflower should not be soft but firm and have the 'bone' in it.

Make a rich white sauce and add the grated cheese. Stir until quite smooth and glossy. Arrange the cauliflower in an oven dish, pour the sauce over it, rasp some hard cheese on top and place in a hot oven for about half an hour until brown. If a more substantial dish is required, six rashers of bacon and three sliced tomatoes may be arranged on top of the cauliflower before placing in the oven.

Cheese and Onions

Cheese and Onions makes a satisfying supper dish and will come to no harm if it is made in the morning and popped into the oven in the evening.

2 *large Spanish onions*	*water*
1 *oz. butter*	4 *oz. cheese*

Slice the onions into a shallow pan, adding a good knob of butter and enough water to keep them from burning. Let them become transparent over a low fire while you finely slice or shred about four ounces of cooking cheese. Leigh Toaster is admirable for this dish (see p. 40). Butter a fireproof dish and lay the onions and cheese in layers until the dish is full, finishing with a layer of cheese. Put into a fairly hot oven for about half an hour or until the cheese has melted and melded with the onions and the top is crisp and brown. Serve hot with crusty brown bread.

Cheese and Onion Pie

4 *oz. cooking cheese*	*salt, black pepper*
1 *large Spanish onion*	*shortcrust pastry (p.* 167)
½ *teacup water*	

Slice the onion into fine rings and stew them gently in a little water. Grate the cheese and when the water has nearly all been absorbed add to the onion and simmer until the cheese has melted.

Line a pie plate with thinly rolled shortcrust pastry; spread with the onion and cheese, season and cover with pastry. Trim

CHEESE AND SAVOURY DISHES

the pastry and pinch the edges to seal in the contents of the plate. Make two small slits in the centre of the piecrust to release the steam, and bake in a hot oven for about thirty minutes. Cheese and onion pie is equally good eaten hot or cold.

Cheese, Potted

In the eighteenth and nineteenth centuries, potted cheeses were very popular. While Cheshire, Cheddar, Gloucester and North Wiltshire cheeses were mainly used, North Wiltshire cheese was considered to be the best. Potted Stilton is still served in London at Simpson's in the Strand.

Mrs. Elizabeth Ray, to whom I owe my thanks for the following recipe, uses a variety of cheeses, but always one pound of mild cheese and one pound of strong and she sometimes substitutes a dry vermouth for the sherry.

2 *lb. cheese*	1 *small glass sherry*
½ *lb. butter*	*ground mace*

Pound the cheese and butter together in a mortar, or if you own an electric mixer the result will be smoother and it is more quickly done. Add the sherry gradually with the mace and when well mixed pot it in small earthenware pots. Pour a little clarified butter over the top and the cheese will keep for weeks in a cool larder. If using Stilton cheese, add port wine instead of sherry.

Cheese Soufflé

1 *oz. butter*	*salt and pepper*
1 *heaped tablespoon flour*	*cayenne*
½ *pint warmed milk*	5 *eggs*
2 *oz. grated cheese*	2 *oz. grated Parmesan cheese*

45

Melt the butter in a saucepan, stir in the flour and cook for a few minutes to break down the starch in the flour. Add the warmed milk slowly, beating all the time to keep the sauce smooth and simmer for five minutes. Stir in the grated cheeses and, away from the fire, four beaten egg yolks. Season to taste with salt, freshly ground pepper and a pinch of cayenne. When the mixture has cooled, fold in the stiffly whipped whites of five eggs. Turn into a one-and-a-half-pint soufflé dish, sprinkle a little extra grated Parmesan cheese on the top and cook in a pre-heated hot oven with the dish standing on an oven sheet about twenty-five minutes. Serve immediately.

Cheese Straws

2 oz. butter	1 egg yolk
2½ oz. flour	½ teaspoon salt
2 oz. Parmesan cheese	pepper
1 oz. Cheddar cheese	cayenne

Sift the salt with the flour and knead in the butter and grated cheeses. Add a good pinch of cayenne and a grind or two of black pepper. Form into a stiff dough with the egg yolk and a little cold water if necessary. Roll out a quarter of an inch thick and cut into strips about four inches long and an eighth of an inch wide. From the trimmings, stamp out some rings about one and a half inches in diameter. Bake in a moderate oven until lightly browned and crisp. This should take ten minutes. Fill each ring with straws and serve warm.

Cheese, Toasted

'Cheddar cheese', says Francatelli who, despite his foreign name, was English born and at one time chief cook to Queen Victoria and later to the Reform Club, 'is allowed to be the richest cheese, and is therefore the best adapted for toasting, from the fact that it is not so liable as other cheeses to become tough and uneatable before it is cold.' His is the following recipe.

Cut the cheese into flakes: put it in a small silver or tin dish. Set the cheese either in the oven or before the fire to toast or melt, and as soon as it becomes thoroughly dissolved, stir it together with a pat of butter, mignonette pepper,* and a little made mustard and let it be eaten instantly with dry toast, or pulled bread.

Cornish Pasty

Quantities for each pasty:

6 *oz. shortcrust pastry (p.* 167)	4 *oz. beef steak*
1 *small potato*	*salt and pepper*
1 *swede*	1 *oz. butter* or *beef dripping*
1 *small onion*	*milk* or *beaten egg for glaze*

The secret of a good Cornish Pasty is to use a shortcrust pastry, uncooked tender steak and plenty of swede, the latter being most important.

For the filling of each pasty you will need a layer of thinly sliced potato, a thick slice of swede, a layer of sliced onion and a top layer of steak cut into small pieces, in the order given. Each layer should be seasoned with salt and pepper and topped with shavings of butter or beef dripping.

Roll out the pastry about a quarter of an inch thick and use a plate to cut into a round of the desired size. Place half the round of pastry over a rolling-pin leaving the other half flat on the board for the filling. When filled, damp the edges with water and pinch them tightly together making a rolled edge so that the pasty cannot open while cooking. Brush the top of the pastry with a little milk or beaten egg to give a slight glaze and make two or three small slits in the centre to

* Mignonette pepper is coarsely ground white peppercorns.

let out the steam when cooking. Lay the pasties on a baking sheet and put them in the centre of a hot oven for twenty minutes, then lower the heat to moderate and cook for forty minutes more.

Devils on Horseback

12 *Carlsbad plums* or *large*   6 *rashers streaky bacon*
   prunes   *hot buttered toast*
red wine

Carlsbad plums are best but good juicy prunes may be used. Soak a dozen large prunes in red wine, overnight if possible, and stew them in the wine for about ten minutes when they should be soft enough to remove the stones. Wrap each prune in half a rasher of bacon and secure with a wooden toothpick, or run them on to a fine skewer. Put in a hot oven for ten minutes when the bacon should be cooked but not overcrisp and the prunes heated through. Serve on hot buttered toast.

Nowadays, when savouries are less common since the hostess is usually the cook, they may be served as an appetizer and handed round with the drinks before dinner. In this case, the toothpicks should be left in, but removed if served at table.

Devilled Soft Roes

½ *lb. soft roes*   *flour*
1½ *oz. butter*   *salt, pepper, cayenne*
lemon juice   *hot buttered toast*

Dip the roes in seasoned flour and shake off the surplus. Heat the butter in a frying-pan until it foams and put in the floured roes. Brown them well on both sides, put a squeeze of lemon juice over the roes, arrange on hot buttered toast and serve at once.

Egg and Cheese

A breakfast dish which has become a firm family favourite.

Boil the eggs for four or five minutes when the yolks should have formed but still be soft. Remove the shells and slice off one end of the eggs so that they stand. Grate some hard cheese and melt in a pan with a little water. Pour over the eggs and serve at once.

Egg and Cheese Savoury

2 *eggs per person*	$\frac{3}{4}$ *pint milk*
$1\frac{1}{2}$ *oz. butter*	*salt and pepper*
1 *tablespoon flour*	3 *oz. grated cheese*

Allow two eggs for each person and boil them for seven minutes then plunge them immediately into cold water. Shell and slice them evenly. An egg-slicer is a useful little tool for this job. Make a white sauce with an ounce and a half of butter, a good tablespoon of flour and three-quarters of a pint of milk. Season with salt and pepper. Add two ounces of grated cheese to the sauce and stir until it has melted. Line the bottom of a fireproof dish with the eggs, pour the sauce over them and grate some cheese on top of the sauce. Place in a hot oven or under the grill until brown and bubbling, and serve with mashed or fried potatoes.

Herring Roes on Toast

2 *herring roes per person*	*melted butter*
hot buttered toast	*paprika*

Allow two herring roes for each person. Poach them in boiling salted water for three minutes then lift out and drain them well. Put them on pieces of hot buttered toast, brush liberally

D

with melted butter and put under a fierce grill for a minute. Dust with paprika before serving. Alternatively, the roes can be dipped in well-seasoned flour and fried in butter before placing them on the toast.

Leek Pie

12 *leeks*	*black pepper*
2 *oz. butter*	*salt*
1 *lb. shortcrust pastry* (*p.* 167)	1 *egg*
	milk or *cream*
2 *rashers bacon*	

Thin leeks are the best to use for this dish.

Wash and drain the leeks having removed the root ends and green tops, leaving only the white part. Slice them not too finely and stew gently in very little water with a good knob of butter until they are nearly cooked.

Line a shallow pie-dish with a layer of thinly rolled pastry and pile in the softened leeks. Pack them closely, together with some finely chopped bacon and a grind or two of black pepper. Cover with the rest of the pastry, pinch the edges to seal and make a slit in the top of the pastry. Bake in a moderate oven until the crust is nearly ready. Beat an egg with a little seasoned milk or cream and pour in through the slit cut in the top of the pie. Put the pie back into the oven for ten minutes to set the custard and serve hot or cold.

Lobscouse (Potato Hash)

2 *lb. shin beef, skirt or cheek*	*water*
3 *lb. potatoes*	*salt and pepper*
2 *lb. onions*	1 *shredded carrot*

Cut the meat into one-inch pieces and put them into a heavy saucepan. Peel and slice the potatoes and onions as finely as

50

possible, shred the carrot and put them all into the pan with the meat. Cover with water, season to taste and cook over a low fire for about three hours or until the contents of the pan have thoroughly melded to the consistency of a thick soup. Serve in soup plates and eat with a spoon.

Marrow, Stuffed

Only young marrows should be used. If freshly cut and tender it should not be necessary to peel them but just scrape them with a sharp knife; it depends very much on the variety, of which there are many.

Cut off the stalk end of the marrow, scoop out the seeds with a dessertspoon. If the marrow is too long to remove all the seeds, it may be cut in half lengthwise and tied together when stuffed. Prepare the stuffing given below and spoon it into the marrow. The vegetable may then be baked or stewed in a rich tomato sauce.

¾ *lb. fresh minced meat*	1 *sprig of mint*
1 *medium-size onion*	*a good pinch of thyme,*
3 *very ripe tomatoes* or	*marjoram and tarragon*
1 *small tin*	4 *tablespoons olive oil*
1 *tablespoon chopped parsley*	*salt and pepper*

Chop the onions finely and cook them for a few minutes in two tablespoons of olive oil and a little water until they have softened. Add the meat, chopped tomatoes and herbs (which should be fresh if possible), season well and stir continuously until the meat turns brown. Test for flavouring and stuff the marrow when cool enough to handle. Put two tablespoons olive oil in a roasting tin with the marrow and cook in a moderate oven, turning occasionally so that it is browned on all sides. One hour should be enough. Baby marrows (courgettes) may be cooked in the same manner.

Marrow Bones

A very old English dish and a favourite with Queen Victoria whose gentility forbade having them served in the bone. The marrow was always removed from the bone and served on toast. They are not often seen nowadays although they did appear as a speciality from time to time on the menu of the Mitre Hotel at Oxford.

Ask your butcher to saw two large fresh marrow bones into three- or four-inch pieces. Scrape and wash them and cover each end with a paste of flour and water to prevent the marrow from escaping. Tie each bone in a cloth and stand them upright in a pan of boiling salted water. Simmer for at least two hours. Take away the cloth and paste, wrap each bone in a small napkin and serve very hot with some crisp toast. The only seasoning required is salt and cayenne pepper. A specially shaped silver spoon is used to scoop the marrow out of the bone.

Rice, Plain Boiled

2 teacups long-grained rice   3 oz. butter
5 teacups hot water   salt

Many cooks noted for their delicious rice puddings find they have little success with plain boiled rice to serve with a variety of savoury dishes. The secret is to choose the right kind of rice and to rinse it well in cold water before cooking. Long rice, which makes unsatisfactory rice puddings, is a must for boiled rice. The round kind will not separate but stick together in a soggy mass.

Melt one ounce of butter in a saucepan, add five teacups of hot water and season with salt. When the water has reached boiling point, shower in two teacups of cleaned long-grain rice and stir once only or the rice may clog. Keep over a brisk fire until the rice swells and the water evaporates. When nearly all the water has been driven off, or absorbed by the rice, cover the saucepan with a clean cloth, put on the pan lid and leave on a very low fire for twenty minutes.

Melt another two ounces of butter and when it bubbles stir it into the rice. Press the rice into a mould and turn out to serve. If you want the rice to be dry and fluffy, leave out the butter.

Scotch Eggs

10 *oz. sausage meat*	1 *beaten egg*
1 *teaspoon chopped parsley*	6 *hard-boiled eggs*
$\frac{1}{2}$ *teaspoon mixed herbs*	*breadcrumbs*
salt and pepper	*cooking fat or oil*

Mix the sausage meat with the herbs and bind with the beaten egg. Season to taste and divide the mixture into six equal portions. Mould the sausage meat carefully round each shelled egg so that it is completely enclosed. Roll each egg in bread-crumbs and fry in deep boiling fat or oil for five minutes or until they are crisp and brown. Drain them well on kitchen paper and serve cold with a salad.

Scotch Woodcock

6 *eggs*	*anchovy fillets*
$1\frac{1}{2}$ *oz. butter*	*capers*
salt and pepper	*hot buttered toast*

Scotch woodcock is simply well-seasoned scrambled eggs on buttered toast with two anchovy fillets crossed on top of the egg and a caper in each quadrant. If anchovy fillets are not available, spread the hot buttered toast with Gentleman's Relish and put the scrambled eggs on this. Serve very hot.

Scrambled Eggs

6 *eggs*   *salt and pepper*
1½ *oz. butter*

Some cooks beat their eggs and I have known others who add milk, but I believe in breaking the eggs direct into the pan with some melted butter. Season them with salt and pepper and stir quickly until nearly set. Remove from the fire and continue to stir for a few seconds when the eggs should be set. Serve at once.

Spinach with Egg

4 *lb. spinach*   2 *oz. grated cheese*
4 *hard-boiled eggs*   *salt and pepper*
½ *pint white sauce (p.* 32)

Clean and rinse the spinach well, removing any tough stalks. If the spinach is young and tender, shake off the surplus water after rinsing and cook in a heavy-bottomed pan without adding more water, taking care that the heat is not too great or it will burn. If the spinach is not so tender it is better to cook it in the continental style in plenty of boiling salted water for about fifteen minutes.

When it is cooked, drain the spinach well and turn into a baking-dish. Slice the hard-boiled eggs, arrange them on top of the spinach and cover with a rich cheese sauce. Sprinkle some grated cheese over the top and brown in a hot oven.

Stuffed Eggs

6 *hard-boiled eggs*   ½ *oz. butter* or 1 *tablespoon*
6 *sardines*   *olive oil*
½ *teaspoon mustard*   *salt and pepper*

Cut six hard-boiled eggs into halves lengthwise and put the yolks into a bowl. Add six sardines to the yolks and mash them roughly with a fork. Add the mustard and the butter or olive oil. Season to taste and fork into the halved egg whites or use a piping funnel for a professional look. Serve on lettuce leaves with quartered tomatoes and cheese.

Welsh Apple Pie

2 *cooking apples*	2 *lb. mashed potatoes*
3 *tomatoes*	1 *oz. grated cheese*
1 *lb. pork sausage meat*	1 *oz. butter*
6 *rashers bacon*	*salt and pepper*

Peel, core and slice the apples. Remove the skin and slice the tomatoes. Line the bottom of a buttered oven-proof dish with the sausage meat and arrange a layer of rashers of bacon over it, then a layer of apples and tomatoes. Season well with salt and pepper and cover with mashed potatoes. Strew the grated cheese on top of the potatoes, add a few shavings of butter and bake in a moderate oven for one hour or until a golden crust has formed.

Welsh Rarebit

A cheese factor in Preston once told me many years ago never to melt a rich Lancashire cheese with milk but always to use water: a tip I have never forgotten.

Melt some well-matured Cheshire, Cheddar or Lancashire cheese (about one and a half ounces per person) with a little water and a grind of pepper. Stir until smooth, pour over slices of buttered toast and brown under the grill.

Welsh Rarebit (2)

Arrange some thin slices of hard cheese (about one and a half ounces per person) on squares of bread previously toasted on one side only. Place under a hot grill until the cheese melts and browns. Serve at once.

Welsh Rarebit (3)

For each person melt a good knob of butter in a saucepan, add a tablespoon of ale, a pinch of salt and a grind of pepper. When just about to boil, grate in about two ounces of cheese to make a thick cream. Stir lightly until blended and on no account let it boil after the cheese has been added. Pour on to slices of hot buttered toast and brown under the grill.

Yorkshire Pudding

Traditionally, Yorkshire pudding was cooked in a tin under the roasting beef and eaten as a separate course with gravy. Nowadays it is usually served with the joint.

For a crisp pudding never use self-raising flour and always bake in a roasting-tin. If glass or earthenware is used the pudding will not rise quickly and the result will be a disappointingly heavy and solid pudding.

4 oz. plain flour	$\frac{1}{4}$ pint milk
$\frac{1}{4}$ teaspoon salt	$\frac{1}{4}$ pint water
1 egg	$1\frac{1}{2}$ oz. beef dripping

Sift the flour and salt into a bowl and make a well in the centre of the flour with a wooden spoon. Break in the egg and mix carefully with the milk and water, until free of lumps. When quite smooth beat well with a wooden spoon until the surface is covered with small bubbles. Melt the dripping in a tin about 10 × 12 inches until really hot. Pour in the batter and cook in the middle of a hot oven for fifteen minutes. If necessary, remove to the top shelf until the pudding puffs and is crisp and golden.

5. Soups

Now that we have mechanical aids in the kitchen such as electric mixers and blenders, much of the weary mashing through a sieve and consequent cleaning up is done away with. We can now produce delicious soups in less than half the time it took our mothers, and economically too, for much of the work of extracting the full flavour from the basic ingredients of a soup can be done with the blender. Some canned soups are an excellent standby and some of the more complicated recipes can rarely be executed at home, but for everyday meals and the economical use of valuable foodstuffs which would otherwise be thrown away, there is nothing like a good home-made soup.

Stock

uncooked meat bones
water

For jellied stock:
veal bones, or *pig's foot*, or
  ½ cow heel

If stock to be used quickly:
1 *onion*
1 *carrot*
1 *stick celery*
faggot of parsley, marjoram, thyme, bayleaf

Many people flinch from making stock because of the complicated work they believe to be involved. Actually, stock is quite easy to make from any bones, fish, poultry or meat, cooked or not, but a really good stock and one which will keep should be made from fresh uncooked bones.

57

Ask the butcher to chop the bones into manageable pieces. Put them into a large pan and cover well with water, unless using a pressure cooker when the instructions for the particular cooker should be followed. Simmer until the bones seem soft and any meat clinging to them falls away. If the stock is to be used quickly, an onion, a carrot and a piece of celery together with a small faggot of parsley stalks, marjoram or thyme and a small bay leaf may be added, but if it is to be kept for several days, then omit the vegetables and herbs as they may turn the stock sour, particularly the onion. If a jellied stock is required, veal bones or a pig's foot or half a cow heel should be added to the meat bones.

Artichoke Soup

This soup is also known as Palestine Soup, which encourages the myth that Jerusalem artichokes have something to do with the Holy Land.

2 *lb. Jerusalem artichokes*	2 *eggs*
2 *oz. butter*	$\frac{1}{4}$ *pint cream*
2 *pints milk*	*salt and pepper*

Peel the artichokes and drop them at once into a bowl of cold water to which has been added one tablespoon of vinegar or the juice of a lemon and two tablespoons flour. Barely cover the artichokes with water and boil until they are soft enough to pass through a sieve or an electric blender. Return to the pan, add the butter and milk, season with salt and pepper and heat. Meanwhile, beat the eggs with one tablespoon of cold water until foamy. Take a ladleful of the hot soup and add it slowly to the beaten eggs, add another ladleful or two, then pour it all back into the pan and stir well. Add the cream last and take care the soup does not boil once the eggs have been added or it will curdle.

Game Soup

This soup may be made with the remains of any cold game.

Break the carcase into pieces, and put the remains, including the skin, into a pan with a few coarsely chopped carrots and onions and a stick or two of celery. Add a faggot of herbs containing parsley, thyme, marjoram and a bay leaf or two. Barely cover with cold water and simmer until the meat leaves the bones. Allow to cool until fit to handle; remove the herbs, all the bones and the skin. Put the rest through an electric blender or fine Mouli with the liquid from the pan. Pour back into the pan, season with salt and pepper, add a small wineglass of sherry and if liked some thin cream. Reheat but do not boil and serve with fried croutons or garnish with chopped parsley.

Green Pea Soup

2 *lb. young peas*	*salt and pepper*
1½ *oz. butter*	*water* or *vegetable stock*
1 *large onion*	1 *pint milk*
mint	3 *or* 4 *tablespoons cream*
1 *teaspoon sugar*	

When the peas are young and the pods are tender, a delicious soup can be made by putting the peas, pods and all, into a pan in which you have melted one ounce of butter and cooked a large grated onion. Add some chopped mint and a teaspoon of sugar and season with salt and freshly ground white pepper. Cover the contents of the pan with water or vegetable stock and bring to boiling point. Simmer gently until the pea pods are soft then remove from the fire and cool. Pass through a sieve or blender and return the purée to the pan. Add one pint of milk, a knob of butter and some fresh cream. Reheat and serve.

Lentil Soup

1 *lb. lentils*	2 *sprays parsley*
2 *onions*	3 *pints water*
2 *carrots*	*salt and pepper*
2 *sprigs thyme*	1 *oz. butter*

Wash the lentils and soak them overnight or at least two hours before they are needed. Put the lentils into a saucepan with the sliced onions and carrot. Add the herbs, season to taste, cover with water and cook for one hour and a half or until the lentils are soft. Pass through a sieve or put through a liquidizer and return to the pan. If the purée is too thick, add hot stock or vegetable water. Stir in the butter and serve with diced fried bread.

Mulligatawny Soup

1 *lb. scrag end of mutton*	2 *oz. butter*
3 *pints water or stock*	1 *tablespoon flour*
1 *apple*	1 *dessertspoon curry powder*
1 *leek*	or *paste*
1 *carrot*	1 *bunch herbs*
2 *slices streaky bacon*	*juice of half a lemon*
1 *stick celery*	*salt and pepper*
1 *stick rhubarb*	

Cut the meat into pieces and cover with water. Bring to the boil and cook until the meat falls from the bones; remove as many of them as you can, keeping the meat on one side. Cut up the vegetables and sauté in butter with the bacon for ten minutes. Add the stock, flour, curry powder or paste, and herbs. Season to taste and bring to the boil. Skim the broth if necessary and cook until the vegetables are soft. Pass all through a sieve and return to the pan. Squeeze in the lemon juice, add the meat cut into small pieces and heat to boiling point. Serve with a separate dish of boiled rice.

This soup is just as good made with a knuckle of veal instead of mutton.

Onion Soup (1)

6 *large onions*	1½ *pints milk*
1 *pint water*	*salt and pepper*
3 *oz. butter*	2 *tablespoons flour*

Chop the onions roughly, put them into a pan with the water and let them stew until quite soft. Add the butter and stir well. Next put in the milk, season with salt and pepper and thicken the soup with the flour mixed to a batter with a little cold milk. Let the soup come nearly to the boil and simmer gently for five minutes.

Onion Soup (2)

6 *large onions*	*salt and pepper*
butter	2 *or* 3 *slices bread*
2 *pints water*	*grated cheese*

Cut the onions into thin slices and cook them in butter until soft and golden brown. Add two pints of water, season with salt and pepper and bring to the boil. Simmer for one hour and just before serving add two or three slices of bread smothered with grated cheese and browned under the grill.

Parsnip Soup

2 *lb. parsnips*	1½ *pints milk*
1 *onion*	*salt and pepper*
3 *oz. butter*	

Peel and cut up the parsnips removing any hard core. Put them into a saucepan with the roughly chopped onion. Barely cover with cold water, add salt and some freshly ground pepper, and boil until the parsnips are soft. Lift them from the pan and rub through a sieve or put through an electric blender. Return to the pan, add the butter and milk and heat to serve. If the soup is too thin, it may be thickened with one heaped tablespoon of flour mixed smoothly with a little milk, and the addition of three or four tablespoons of cream enriches the soup enormously. Garnish with chopped parsley.

Potato Soup

2 *lb. potatoes*	*salt and pepper*
1 *large leek*	1½ *pints milk*
2 *onions*	¼ *pint cream*
2 *oz. butter*	*chives*
water	

Prepare and cut up the vegetables using only the white part of the leek and put them into a saucepan with the butter. Let them cook about ten minutes taking care they do not colour. Add enough water to cover the vegetables, season with salt and pepper and cook for about three-quarters of an hour or until the vegetables are soft enough to rub through a sieve. Return the purée to the pan and stir in the milk. Bring to boiling point and remove from the fire. Stir in the cream, sprinkle the top with some chopped chives, and serve at once.

Scotch Broth (sometimes called Barley Broth)

1 *lb. scrag end mutton*	2 *onions*
4 *tablespoons pearl barley*	1 *stick celery*
3 *pints water or stock*	*pepper and salt*
1 *carrot*	1 *dessertspoon chopped parsley*
1 *turnip*	

Discard any superfluous fat and cut the meat into pieces. Wash the barley and put it with the bones and meat into a heavy saucepan, add water and bring to the boil. Skim carefully and simmer the broth for two hours, or half an hour in a pressure cooker will be enough. Remove the bones and add the vegetables peeled, scraped, washed and cut into dice. Season with salt and pepper and simmer until the vegetables are cooked. Sprinkle in the chopped parsley and serve hot.

Tomato Soup

2 lb. ripe tomatoes	1½ pints milk
2 onions	salt and pepper, sugar
½ pint water	1 oz. flour
2 oz. butter	¼ pint cream

Dip the tomatoes in hot water for half a minute when the skin will come away easily. Chop them roughly and put them into a pan with the sliced onions, cover with water and bring to the boil. Simmer for about one hour or until the tomatoes and onions are soft; rub through a sieve to remove the seeds. Put the purée back into the pan with the butter. Add the milk and season with salt, pepper and sugar. Reheat but do not boil. Thicken with the flour mixed smooth with water or milk, adjust seasoning and just before serving, add the cream. A dessertspoon of tomato paste improves both colour and flavour.

Vegetable Soup

2 onions	1 turnip
3 tablespoons olive oil	1 stick celery
2 oz. butter	2 cloves garlic
1 leek	2 bay leaves
2 carrots	parsley
1 potato	mint

63

marjoram

6 *ripe tomatoes* or 1 *tin of*
   tomatoes

2 *quarts of water* or *stock*

sugar, salt and pepper

3 *tablespoons semolina*

1 *wineglass red wine*

Chop the onions and put them to soften in a large saucepan
with the olive oil, butter and one cup of water. Cut the rest
of the vegetables up small and chop the herbs finely. Add to
the contents of the pan with the sliced garlic cloves and stir
for five minutes. Add the skinned and chopped tomatoes,
water, one teaspoon of sugar, season with salt and pepper and
lastly add the red wine and semolina. Simmer until the
vegetables are soft. The soup may be eaten as it is or put
through a sieve: it is a matter of taste.

White Vegetable Soup

2 *lb. vegetables*

2 *oz. butter*

salt and pepper

1½ *pints milk*

diced fried bread

Cut two pounds of any vegetables to hand (onions, turnips,
potatoes, parsnips, artichokes, celery, etc.) in small pieces and
put them into a heavy saucepan. Add the butter and season
with salt and pepper. Cover with water. Bring to the boil and
cook until the vegetables are soft. Pass through a sieve or an
electric blender and return to the pan. Add one and a half
pints of milk and heat until nearly boiling. If the soup is too
thin, add one tablespoon of flour mixed smooth with a little
milk. Stir well and serve hot garnished with diced fried bread.
A little cream added before serving enriches this soup enormously.

6. Fish

Despite the fact that we are an island people and live in a land rich in rivers, lakes and streams and where fishing is a national sport and pastime, as a nation we are singularly conservative about fish. Not only the fish we buy, but how we cook it.

It is said that in the late seventeenth century as much money was spent on fish as on meat. Elizabeth I ordained that certain days should be fast days; the legal obligation to observe them did not survive the Civil War but the fish-eating habit lasted well into the eighteenth century and London fish-mongers as a class were wealthy and important citizens.

Boiled Fish

Few realize that fish should never actually be boiled. It is far too fierce a method of cooking such a delicate food and will only result in torn skin, broken flesh and an unappetizing dish. Boiled fish is only a manner of speaking and it should be poached gently and carefully in a court bouillon of water in which a few herbs and vegetables have already been cooked. Lemon juice or wine added to the water ensure a firm flesh. Salt, carrot, onion, a small bunch of parsley and one of celery leaves, fennel and a few crushed peppercorns make a good stock and should be removed before lowering the fish into the liquid and poaching gently for a short while (five to ten minutes per pound depending on thickness, or ten to fifteen minutes for small fish; cooking times are the same for steamed fish). The fish should be allowed to remain in the water for a few minutes before it is lifted out. Cooked in this way, the fish remains whole and presentable. The stock makes a good basis for fish soup, except salmon stock which is too oily and strong-tasting for most people.

Fried Fish

Traditional English fish and chips (see potatoes, p. 153) are best deep fried in fat or vegetable oil. At least a pint of oil should be heated slowly in a deep pan until the bubbling has stopped and a light haze rises from the surface (375° F). Cod, haddock or hake are more commonly used but plaice or whiting are also excellent. Coat the fish either in beaten egg and breadcrumbs or in a thick batter and cook, two or three pieces at a time, for five to ten minutes depending on the size.

For a thick coating of batter:

4 oz. plain flour	1 egg
2 teaspoons baking powder	¼ pint milk
salt and pepper	

Sift the dry ingredients into a bowl. Put the egg and half the milk into a well in the centre and mix gradually into the flour. Beat lightly until smooth, then add the rest of the milk.

Small fish, such as herrings, may be coated in beaten egg and breadcrumbs and shallow-fried in butter.

Cod

Cod is of the same family as haddock, whiting and hake and all these fish may be cooked in the same manner. A codling may be poached in a court bouillon (see Boiled Fish, p. 65) and the liquor makes a good soup.

Grilled or fried cod steaks require a good sauce, such as black butter, caper, parsley or shrimp sauce (see Chapter 2), as cod itself has not much flavour.

Cod Steaks with Onion and Tomato

6 *cod steaks*	4 *ripe tomatoes*
salt and pepper	*chopped parsley*
lemon juice	1 *onion*
butter	

Arrange the cod steaks in a well-oiled or buttered baking-dish. Season with salt, pepper and a squeeze of lemon juice. Smother the fish with roughly chopped ripe tomatoes, finely chopped parsley and a grated onion. Add more salt, pepper and butter and bake in a moderately hot oven for three-quarters of an hour.

Cod in Sherry

Any fish which will cut into steaks, cod, halibut, turbot, etc., will do for this dish.

6 *fish steaks*	*lemon juice*
4 *oz. butter*	1½ *oz. flour*
2 *small onions*	4 *tablespoons sherry*
4 *oz. mushrooms*	½ *pint milk*
salt and pepper	1 *tablespoon chopped parsley*

Season the wiped and trimmed steaks with salt, pepper and lemon juice. Slice the onions finely and sauté them in two ounces of butter until soft but not brown. Lay them in a fireproof casserole and sauté the sliced mushrooms in any butter left from cooking the onions. Put the steaks on the bed of onions and cover with the mushrooms. Melt two ounces of butter and add the flour and sherry then the milk and stir until thickened. Season, add the parsley, pour over the fish and bake for half an hour in a moderate oven.

Crab

Crabs are messy things to prepare attractively for the table and given a good fishmonger and time, he will do it for you. If you have to do your own, then choose a heavy cock crab which can be recognized by its larger claws. They are at their best from May to August. If selecting a crab which has been cooked, take it by the claws and shake it from side to side. If it rattles, then it is probably watery and therefore of inferior quality. Preference should be given to those which have a rough shell and large claws.

If the crab is alive, drop it into salted boiling water and reheat quickly to boiling point. Cook for twenty minutes, drain and rinse in cold water. On no account leave the crab standing in water. Twist off the claws and the flaps and separate the upper shell from the lower, or apron. Remove the intestines and stomach which is placed near the head. Pick out all the meat from body and claws, clean the deep shell and mix the meat with a dressing of wine vinegar, olive oil and a pinch of mustard to taste. Put the mixture back in the shell as neatly as possible and garnish with chopped parsley.

A crab prepared by a good fishmonger will be more elaborate than this but will not taste any better.

Crayfish

A species of small fresh-water lobster found in many streams and rivers in the British Isles, crayfish are considered a great delicacy in France. They should not be confused with crawfish, the clawless spiny lobster of the sea. Dropped into boiling salted water for a few minutes they will turn pink and when cool enough to handle the flesh may be picked from the shell and served with a dressing of olive oil and lemon juice.

Eels, Stewed

Skin and clean two pounds of eel or ask the fishmonger to prepare them for you. Cut the fish into two-inch lengths and put them in a saucepan with a little salt, the juice of half a lemon, and a tablespoon of chopped parsley. Barely cover with water and simmer gently in a covered pan for about one hour. Remove the fish to a serving dish and keep warm. Blend into the liquor one ounce of butter and one ounce of flour previously well creamed together. Stir until smooth. Taste for seasoning then pour over the eels, garnish with chopped parsley and serve hot.

Stewed eels are equally good with an anchovy sauce which is made in the same manner but using anchovy essence instead of parsley. In this case, garnish the dish with a little paprika sprinkled over the top.

Finnan Haddock

The story is told that in the fishing village of Findon in Scotland a building in which a quantity of wood was stored caught fire. After the fire was extinguished, it was found that some haddock left in the building became golden brown in colour and on being cooked had a delicious flavour. Further experiments were made and so it was that Findon haddock became famous, though the name Findon changed and is popularly known as 'Finnan' or 'Finney'.

Finnan Haddock, Poached

2–3 *lb. Finnan haddock*   *butter*
1 *teacup milk*   *black pepper*

Put the haddock in a shallow pan, add the milk, two or three pieces of butter and some freshly ground black pepper. Poach gently for five or ten minutes according to the size of the fish. Some people like to serve poached eggs on the fish but this is a matter of taste.

Haddock Scallops

A quickly made dish, useful for a first course, a light luncheon or a supper dish.

1½ *lb. Finnan haddock*	2 *oz. butter*
milk	2 *oz. Parmesan cheese*
2 *eggs*	2 *oz. breadcrumbs*
black pepper	

Place the fish in a shallow pan and barely cover with milk. Bring to the boil, remove from the fire and allow the fish to cool in the liquor. Remove the skin and bones and flake the fish. Beat the eggs well until frothy, add the liquor in which the fish has been cooked, then the flaked fish and season well with black pepper. Put the fish into deep scallop shells and have the breadcrumbs and grated cheese ready. Sprinkle half the amount of cheese over the fish then a fairly thick layer of breadcrumbs and finally the rest of the cheese. Dot with butter and place under the grill until the cheese has melted and the top is golden and the fish cooked through.

Haddock Soufflé (Windsor Soufflé)

1 *lb. Finnan haddock*	2 *oz. grated cheese*
¾ *pint milk*	*black pepper*
1½ *oz. butter*	6 *egg whites*
1½ *oz. flour*	

Trim the haddock and simmer gently in milk, or milk and water for ten minutes. Strain, remove the skin and bones and flake the fish with a fork. Melt the butter in a saucepan, add the flour and make a sauce with the liquid in which the fish has been cooked. Add the cheese, flaked haddock and a generous grate of black pepper. Fold in the beaten egg whites and pour into a well-buttered soufflé dish. Place in the centre of a hot oven and leave undisturbed for twenty minutes, when the soufflé should be well risen and golden on top. Serve at once.

Halibut

A somewhat coarser and larger fish than the turbot, halibut is usually sold in steaks, although baby halibut is sometimes obtainable weighing about three or four pounds when it may be poached like turbot.

Halibut, Baked

6 *halibut steaks*   *chopped parsley*
salt and black pepper $\frac{1}{2}$ *lemon*
butter

Put the halibut steaks into a buttered fireproof dish. Season with salt and black pepper, add some shavings of butter, chopped parsley and the juice of half a lemon. Place in a moderate oven for three-quarters of an hour when the fish should be cooked. Baste once or twice during this time or the fish may be dry. Serve with mashed potatoes.

Halibut with Shrimps

2 *lb. halibut*   *nutmeg*
salt and pepper   *butter*
$\frac{1}{2}$ *pint picked shrimps*   1 *teacup milk*

Place a thick halibut steak in a well-buttered baking-dish.

Season with salt and pepper and add the picked shrimps. Grate in a little nutmeg, put some small pieces of butter over the fish and add the milk. Cover with foil and bake in a moderate oven for three-quarters of an hour or until the fish is cooked.

Alternatively, bake the halibut with butter, make a rich shrimp sauce (p. 30) and pour over the fish when it is cooked. Brown under a hot grill and serve at once.

Herrings, Grilled

Split and remove the centre bone and as many others as you can see and have time for. Open them flat, dab each fish with butter, season and with the skin uppermost place under a hot grill. Turn once and serve piping hot. If preferred, the herrings may be breadcrumbed and fried in fresh butter. Grilled herrings are usually served with a mustard sauce (p. 28). Many cooks prefer coarse oatmeal to breadcrumbs.

Herrings, Kippered

Kippers have long been an alternative to the bacon and egg breakfast of the British. Care should be taken in buying kippers. If they are very yellow it is more than likely that they have been dyed as well as smoked and it may be necessary to scald them in hot water for a minute or two before cooking.

Manx kippers are a rare delight. Small, lightly smoked and of a delicate pale colour in contrast to the often highly coloured Yarmouth kippers, they are obtainable only during a very short season. Trawled by fishermen from Peel in the Isle of Man when the young herrings are running in the Irish Sea from June to September, it is only the people of Peel who hold the secret of curing the Manx kipper.

Wipe the kippers with a damp cloth and put them under the grill or in the top of a hot oven with a good dab of butter on each one. Cook for about six to eight minutes, until the kippers are heated through and serve at once.

Bloaters, another variety of smoked herring, should be slit open, the bones and roes removed and grilled in the same way. Fry the roes in butter and serve with the bloaters.

Herrings, Soused

Remove the heads, tails and backbone from the herrings, salt them well, and roll them up tightly packing them close together in an earthenware dish. If liked, a thin slice of onion may be wrapped in each herring. Put in plenty of peppercorns and nearly cover with malt vinegar. Bake gently until cooked, about one hour. Let them go cold and serve in the dish in which they have been cooked.

Soused mackerel or trout can also be prepared in the same way but packed close together without removing the bones or rolling them.

Lobster

One of the most highly rated of all shell fish, a cock lobster is regarded as being better for eating than the hen which is used for garnishes and sauces because of the coral. The cock is recognized by the narrowness of the tail and the stiffness of the two uppermost fins. Lobsters should be chosen by weight rather than size. A small lobster, heavy for its size, is the best buy. Choose one weighing between two and three pounds.

To boil a live lobster, put it head first into a large pan of fast boiling water. It will be killed instantly and this is the most humane way of doing it. Cover the pan and simmer gently for twenty minutes to half an hour at most, according to the size of the lobster. The flesh tends to be stringy if it is overcooked. Remove from the boiling water and plunge the lobster into cold water for an instant, then place it on a dish to cool.

Lobster with Rice and Curry Sauce

This recipe is equally good for fresh prawns or crawfish.

1 *lobster*	½ *teaspoon saffron*
1 *tablespoon sultanas*	1 *flat teaspoon curry powder*
1 *small glass sherry*	or *paste*
2 *oz. butter*	½ *teaspoon paprika*
salt and pepper	4 *oz. patna rice*

Remove all the flesh from a cooked lobster and cut it into chunky pieces. Crush the shells and claws, barely cover them with water and simmer for half an hour. Meanwhile, soak the sultanas in the sherry until they are nice and plump. Melt the butter in a shallow pan and when it is foaming toss in the lobster. Season with salt, pepper and spices and heat thoroughly. Strain the lobster stock into the pan and as soon as it boils throw in the rice. Stir with a silver fork from time to time until the rice has absorbed the liquor. For the Curry Sauce, see p. 22.

Mackerel, Baked

Good fresh mackerel are easily recognized. Their bodies are stiff, gills red, eyes bright and of a good colour. Of all fish, mackerel must be very fresh.

One of the nicest ways of cooking them is to put each cleaned fish into an oiled or buttered piece of foil. Season well with salt and freshly ground pepper and if liked a dessertspoon of white wine. Any finely chopped mixed herbs may also be used. Enclose the fish, complete with heads, and twist the ends of the foil tightly so that the juices are retained. Cook for half an hour in a moderate oven and serve as they are, each fish in its foil.

Mackerel, Grilled

Split the mackerel down the back, season with salt and freshly ground pepper and lightly oil the fish all over. Place under the hot grill and turn them over when browned on one side. When cooked, remove to a hot serving-dish and serve with the following sauce poured over them.

Brown two ounces of butter in a shallow pan, add two table-spoons of tarragon vinegar, and one of Harvey's sauce. Mix well and add one tablespoon of chopped capers.

Mackerel, Poached

Allow one mackerel for each person and ask your fishmonger to clean them but to leave the heads on.

Lower the fish into a wide shallow pan containing boiling salted water and let the water bubble gently until the fish are cooked (about ten minutes). Lift the fish carefully without breaking from the water and transfer them to a heated serving-dish. Send to table with a rich fennel or parsley sauce (p. 29).

Mussels, Pickled

6 *pints mussels* 1½ *pints malt vinegar*
1 *pint water* 1 *oz. pickling spice*
salt

Scrape the mussels clean and wash them well in plenty of water. Put them into a pan containing one pint of boiling salted water. Cover to cook until the mussels have opened. Allow them to cool a little and remove the beard by holding the shell between the finger and thumb of one hand and the beard in the other. Close the shell and pull the beard away, then remove the mussels from the shells. Have ready a serving-bowl containing one and a half pints of malt vinegar which has been boiled together with one ounce of pickling spice. When cold, strain the vinegar into the serving-bowl. As the mussels are cleaned, throw them into the marinade. Stand for twenty-four hours and serve cold.

Note: Discard any opened mussels before cooking and any that do not open during cooking.

Salmon

Salmon is at its best cooked very simply. It may be poached or baked. If cooking a whole salmon or salmon trout, the fish should be put into a fish kettle containing cold water and vinegar or lemon juice or a court bouillon (see Boiled Fish, p. 65). Bring it to the boil, draw aside from the fire and poach it very gently allowing five minutes to the pound for a four-pound fish. Let it cool in the water. If it is to be eaten hot it should be left for fifteen minutes before lifting it from the water.

A piece of salmon is better baked than boiled. Season and wrap it in buttered paper or foil and seal it well. Place the fish in a fireproof dish and bake it in a moderate oven for half to three-quarters of an hour. If it is to be eaten cold, leave it in the paper until required. The salmon will be found to be delicate, succulent and full of flavour.

Hollandaise, caper, cucumber or parsley sauce may be served with hot boiled salmon but the classic way of serving cold salmon is with mayonnaise (for Sauces see Chapter 2).

Salmon Steaks

The steaks should be cut fairly thick or they will dry up in cooking. They may be grilled with a generous knob of butter on each steak which browns nicely without drying the fish, or they may be wrapped in individual pieces of foil and baked in the oven for twenty to thirty minutes. Serve with new potatoes, green peas and cucumber salad or a rich parsley sauce (p. 29).

Salmon Trout

Salmon trout is a sea trout with the same habits as salmon, and spawns in fresh water. It resembles salmon in that it has a tender pink flesh and a similar but more delicate flavour. It is also less rich and oily than salmon. Poach very gently in water and vinegar or wine or a court bouillon (see Boiled Fish, p. 65) allowing five minutes to the pound of fish and allow to cool in the liquid in which it has been cooked. Serve with mayonnaise (p. 26).

Scallops and Bacon

Allow two scallops per person and ask your fishmonger to clean them for you. If they are really fresh, they may be kept up to three days if placed in a bowl of tap water, which must be changed each day. They will plump up and none of the delicate flavour will be lost but they must be absolutely fresh when bought.

12 *scallops*	1 *tablespoon lemon juice*
4 *slices streaky bacon*	1 *wineglass sherry*
1 *tablespoon chopped parsley*	*salt and pepper*
1½ *oz. butter*	

Clean the scallops and cut each one into three pieces. Cut the bacon into small pieces and brown lightly in half the butter. Dust the scallops with salt and pepper and add to the bacon together with the lemon juice and the rest of the butter. Cook for five minutes until the scallops are tender then stir in the chopped parsley. Remove the scallops to a hot serving-dish, swill the sherry round the pan and let it bubble for a minute. Pour it over the scallops and serve very hot.

Scallops with Wine and Mushrooms

12 *scallops* $\frac{1}{2}$ *pint milk*
$\frac{1}{2}$ *lb. mushrooms*   2 *tablespoons double cream*
4 *oz. butter*   *salt and freshly ground black*
2 *oz. flour*   *pepper to taste*
1 *wineglass of dry white wine*

Cut the scallops into pieces about one inch square. Wipe and slice the mushrooms, stalks and all. Make a thick white sauce with half the butter, the flour, wine and milk and at the same time sauté the mushrooms in the rest of the butter. Mushrooms soak up a lot of butter so you may need to add a little extra to prevent them from drying. When the sauce has bubbled long enough to get rid of the taste of flour, add the mushrooms and any liquor left in the pan. Stir well, add the cream, the scallops and season to taste. Pour it all into a shallow baking-dish, well buttered, cover tightly with foil and cook in a moderate oven for twenty-five minutes. Garnish with parsley and serve with creamy mashed potatoes.

Shrimps

If you are lucky enough to buy fresh-boiled picked shrimps, eat them as they are with salt, pepper, olive oil and vinegar and some thinly sliced brown bread and butter.

Shrimps, Potted

1 *gill picked shrimps*   3 *oz. butter*
salt and black pepper $\frac{1}{4}$ *nutmeg*

Melt two ounces of butter in an open pan. Toss in one gill

of picked shrimps, a good pinch of salt and freshly ground black pepper to taste. Grate in a quarter of nutmeg and sauté the shrimps until they turn pink and have absorbed all the butter. Pot and press down. When cold, seal with melted butter and they will keep a week in a cool place.

Skate

At one time, skate was one of the cheapest of fish and used mainly in fish and chip shops. However, it seems to be coming up in the world of fashionable small eating places. It is rather a bother to prepare owing to its glutinous fins but if he isn't too busy a fishmonger will prepare it for you. It is usually sold by the wing which should weigh about two pounds and is improved enormously in flavour if left to soak in salted water and lemon juice for a couple of hours. Skate and Dover sole are the only fish I know of that are better not eaten fresh from the sea.

Poach the fillets in milk seasoned with salt, pepper and a knob of butter, or in simmering water with salt and a faggot of herbs. Add a few chopped capers to black butter sauce (p. 18).

Skate with Orange

2 *lb. skate*	1 *teaspoon sugar*
faggot of herbs	1 *teaspoon chopped parsley*
1 *medium-size onion*	1 *teaspoon chopped thyme*
2 *oz. butter*	*salt, pepper*
2 *oranges*	*dash of wine vinegar*

Poach the skate in water with a faggot of herbs for thirty minutes. Drain very well; remove the skin and bones and put the fish in a casserole. Chop the onion finely, melt half the butter in a small frying-pan and cook the onion until it is soft.

Peel one orange and slice into rounds and put them in the frying-pan with the rest of the butter. Dust with sugar and fry rather quickly until the orange slices are heated through. Add the juice of the other orange, the herbs, seasoning and vinegar, bring to the boil and pour over the fish which has been kept hot.

Sole

There is no finer fish than the Dover sole. The French have invented many ways of cooking it and a variety of sauces to go with it. Expertly fried or grilled and served with half a lemon it takes a lot of beating. Serve one small or medium-size sole per person; one large sole filleted will serve two people.

Sole with White Wine

For two people:

  1 *large sole*   1 *tablespoon chopped parsley*
  salt and pepper   1 *wineglass white wine or*
  butter   *the juice of* 1 *lemon*

Skin the sole and place it in a well-buttered baking-dish. Season with salt and pepper. Add a few small pieces of butter and sprinkle one tablespoon of chopped parsley over the fish. Pour in a wineglass of white wine and place in a moderate oven for about twenty minutes. Alternatively use lemon juice.

Sole with Cheese

Prepare the sole as in the preceding recipe but instead of the parsley sprinkle two tablespoons of grated cheese over the fish. When the cheese has melted, brown quickly under the grill. The combination of wine and cheese with the sole is superb.

Sole with Shrimps and Mussels

3 *large soles* or 1½ *lb. fillets*	1 *wineglass white wine*
1 *gill picked shrimps* or	1 *tablespoon flour*
prawns	½ *oz. butter*
1 *gill cooked mussels*	½ *teacup milk* or *cream*

Choose large soles and ask the fishmonger to fillet them. Roll the fillets and secure them with wooden toothpicks. Arrange the fillets in an oven dish, add the picked shrimps or prawns, the mussels and a wineglass of white wine. Cook in a moderate oven for twenty minutes. Make a white sauce with the flour, butter and milk or cream. Combine this sauce with the liquor in the dish, season and pour it over the fish and serve.

Trout

All varieties of trout are good either grilled, poached in a little vinegar and water or wrapped in foil and baked. A single folded leek leaf holds a trout nicely for grilling and imparts an unusual flavour.

Trout with Fennel

6 *trout*	1 *wineglass white wine*
fennel	1 *oz. butter*
salt and black pepper	

Put some finely sliced fennel into a well-buttered baking-dish. Season the trout lightly with salt and a grind of black pepper and lay them in the dish on the fennel. Moisten with white wine. Strew the fish with chopped fennel leaves. Cover and let them cook gently in a moderate oven. When the trout are cooked remove them to a serving-dish. Reduce the liquor in which they have been cooked, thicken with butter, adjust the seasoning and pour over the trout.

Trout, Grilled

6 *trout*	*lemon juice*
melted butter	*chopped parsley*

Season the trout lightly. Brush them with melted butter and lemon juice and place them on a very hot grill which has also been brushed with butter and lemon juice. This is done to prevent the fish from sticking to the grill and presenting an unsightly appearance at table. When cooked on one side turn the fish over and cook until brown. Serve with melted butter and chopped parsley.

Turbot

A large flat fish with a firm rather glutinous flesh, turbot was considered a great delicacy by the Victorians who believed it was better to steam than to poach it. Apart from a chicken turbot when one usually buys the whole fish, turbot is sold in cuts.

Poached in milk or steamed (see Boiled Fish, p. 65), serve it with a shrimp, lobster, egg or caper sauce (see Chapter 2). It is also very good cooked with wine (see below).

Turbot with Wine

4 *lb. turbot*	*chopped parsley*
salt and pepper	*butter*
nutmeg	1 *wineglass white wine*

Put the fish into a buttered fireproof dish, season with salt, pepper and a grate of nutmeg. Smother the fish with chopped parsley, some pieces of butter and pour into the dish a large wineglass of white wine. Put it into a moderate oven until the fish is cooked, about three-quarters of an hour. Serve it in the dish in which it has been cooked.

Turbot, Poached

4 *lb. turbot*	*milk*
water	4 *slices lemon*

Turbot should be poached in a liquor of three parts of water to one part of milk and four slices of lemon from which the pips and rind have been removed. It should be freshly made and the fish lowered into the hot liquor. Allow ten minutes to a pound of fish but thirty minutes should be enough for four pounds. Allow the fish to cool a little in the liquor before serving.

Whitebait

The fry of the common herring, freshly caught and properly cooked, whitebait are a great delicacy. Allow two pounds for six people. They should be rinsed well in salted water, then thoroughly drained. When they are ready to cook, put them into a floured kitchen cloth, shake them well so that they are completely and evenly floured, shake off the surplus flour and fry them quickly in very hot oil until lightly browned and crisp. The oil must be hot (375° F) when the fish are put in or they will turn out greasy instead of crisp and dry. As they cook, lift them from the pan, drain on kitchen paper and keep hot to serve.

Fish Cakes

1 *lb. fish (see recipe)*	1 *egg*
3 *or* 4 *potatoes*	*milk*
salt and pepper	*butter*
dash of Worcestershire sauce	*breadcrumbs*
1 *tablespoon chopped parsley*	

Poach about one pound of cod, hake, whiting or salmon. Peel and boil three or four potatoes. There should be more fish than potatoes. Remove all the skin and bones from the fish and flake it into a mixing-bowl. Pound it well and add the potatoes having put them through a ricer or mashed them smoothly. Add salt, freshly ground pepper, a dash of Worcestershire sauce (except when using salmon) and the chopped parsley. Bind the mixture with a well-beaten egg and add a little milk if the mixture seems too dry. Mould the fish into cakes about three inches in diameter and half an inch thick. Brush them with melted butter and dip them quickly into some dried breadcrumbs. Have ready a deep pan of cooking oil and when just smoking hot (390° F) put in the cakes and fry for two to three minutes until deep golden. Garnish with parsley and serve with shrimp or egg sauce (see Chapter 2).

Fish Omelette

4 *oz. cooked fish*	4 *eggs*
¼ *pint white sauce (p.* 32)	*Worcestershire sauce*
2 *tablespoons chopped parsley*	*salt and pepper*

Remove all the skin and bones from the fish. Flake the fish and mix with the white sauce and parsley. Add the well-beaten eggs, a few drops of Worcestershire sauce and season to taste. Pour the mixture into a well-oiled omelette pan and cook until it is firm. Place under the grill for a few minutes until nicely browned and serve with a green salad.

Fish Pie

2 *lb. cooked fish*	2 *tablespoons chopped parsley*
2 *oz. butter*	*salt and pepper*
3 *tablespoons flour*	2 *lb. mashed potatoes*
½ *pint milk*	2 *tablespoons grated cheese*

Remove all the skin and bones from the fish and flake it finely. Make a white sauce with the butter, flour and milk and add the fish and the parsley. Season well with salt and pepper. Butter a baking-dish and put in the fish. Cover with mashed potatoes and grate the cheese over the potatoes. Cook in the top of a moderate oven for about half an hour or until well browned.

Fish Soufflé

Poached cod, hake, fresh haddock or salmon are all good fish to use.

8 *oz. cooked fish*	*essence of anchovy*
1 *oz. butter*	4 *eggs*
¼ *pint milk*	*salt and pepper*
1 *oz. flour*	

Remove any skin or bone from the fish and flake the fish as finely as possible. Melt the butter in a saucepan, add the flour and heat over a low fire. Add the milk slowly, beating all the time to keep the sauce smooth. Add the fish, beaten egg yolks, anchovy essence and season with salt and pepper. Draw aside to cool, meanwhile whisk the egg whites stiffly and fold lightly into the cooled mixture. Pour into a buttered soufflé dish and cook in a moderately hot oven for twenty-five minutes. Serve at once with a mixed green salad (page 160).

Kedgeree

Originally an Indian dish, kedgeree makes a useful supper dish. It may be prepared in advance and is a good way of using up cold fish. Salmon is considered by many to be the best fish to use but, while many cooks deplore the use of Finnan haddock, for my taste it is the best.

4 oz. long-grained rice   2 hard-boiled eggs
2 oz. butter   salt and pepper
8 oz. cooked fish   cayenne pepper

Prepare the rice according to the recipe given on page 52 and put it into a large saucepan with the butter, flaked fish and chopped hard-boiled eggs. Season and when really hot turn on to a serving-dish. Dust with cayenne pepper and serve at once.

7. Meat

Since the days when an ox was roasted whole in the market square and castle courtyard, the roast beef of old England has been a byword and a cut off the joint and two veg synonymous with English cooking. Scotch beef, Welsh and Southdown lamb at their best are unsurpassable.

Sir Henry Thompson, writing in 1888, says 'The Englishman loves the flavour of three- or four-year-old mutton (unhappily almost a tradition now), mature beef, the wildest game, both winged and ground; and he cares not how little of "sauce" is supplied—he demands only "gravy"; so that these are in fine condition, sufficiently, not over-kept, and simply cooked, for the most part carefully roasted'.

The pleasant and popular tale that the merry monarch Charles II knighted the Roast of Beef at a jolly party at Chingford, Essex, after a day's hunting in Epping Forest is unlikely to be the true origin of the word 'sirloin'. Some devotees of the Sir Loin story believe that it was James I who in 1617 dubbed the roast when he stayed at Hoghton Tower in Lancashire. Indeed, the National Beef Council of America has recently presented a plaque to commemorate the event, which was unveiled by Sir Cuthbert de Hoghton, one of whose ancestors entertained King James.

Much more likely is it that the word sirloin derives from two Norman French words 'sur' and 'loin' but whatever the origin of the word, this cut of beef is undoubtedly the most tender and succulent of all for roasting and appropriately expensive. It should be roasted simply but carefully.

BEEF

Roast Beef

Choose a well-hung joint of sirloin or ribs of beef weighing not less than five to seven pounds. Dredge lightly with flour and put to cook in a hot oven until the juices are sealed within the meat and it begins to sizzle. Lower the heat and cook until the meat is tender. When done, the meat should be well-browned and crisp outside and underdone and pink within. One hour and a half should be enough for this size roast, longer if not liked underdone.

Horseradish sauce (p. 24) and gravy made from the juices in the roasting-tin are usual accompaniments and, of course, Yorkshire pudding (p. 56). In my family we always slice a Spanish onion and marinade it in malt vinegar with a teaspoon of sugar, a pinch of salt and pepper and serve it with roast beef, hot or cold.

Beef Cooked in Beer

This method of cooking beef is very good for tough meat. It may be cooked as a pot roast, or in the oven when it is better to use an earthenware baking-dish.

joint of beef	*½ teaspoon pickling spice*
2 large onions	*bunch of any mixed herbs*
1 breakfast cup of vinegar	*beer (mild)*
1 tablespoon treacle	

Tie the meat into shape and put into an earthenware dish. Chop the onion, skins and all, and spread over the meat, put in the bunch of herbs and pour over it the vinegar and

88

treacle. Let it stand all day or overnight in a cool place. Pour in enough mild beer to cover the meat and bring to the boil. Skim carefully and simmer slowly for two or three hours until the meat is quite tender. Lift out the meat and serve on a platter with plain boiled potatoes and hot boiled beetroot.

Brisket

One of the cheaper cuts of beef which, providing you like fat, makes a delicious joint if properly cooked. It is excellent pressed and eaten cold and a good bowl of dripping is always obtained from a piece of brisket, making it a very good buy.

Braised Brisket

4-6 *lb. brisket*	*salt and pepper*
12 *shallots* or *small onions*	1 *teacup water*
3 *leeks*	*suet dumplings* (*p.* 184)
6 *young carrots*	

Put the brisket into a self-basting roasting-tin. Surround the meat with the shallots or small onions, the sliced leeks and the carrots. Season with salt and pepper, add one teacup of water and cook in a very slow oven for at least three hours or until the meat is beginning to come away from the bones. One hour before the meat is ready add some small suet dumplings. Remove the meat to a hot dish, surround it with the cooked vegetables and dumplings and serve with plain boiled potatoes.

Roast Brisket

Choose a piece of brisket weighing not less than four pounds. Put the joint into a roasting-tin, preferably a self-baster, with half a teacup of water and place in a hot oven for half an hour, then reduce the heat and braise slowly for four hours or until the meat is cooked. Drain off the surplus fat before making the gravy.

To serve cold

Remove the bones from the meat while it is still warm. Put the meat into a mould, press down and leave overnight, well weighted. Turn out to serve with a salad and pickles.

Silverside of Beef

4 *lb. silverside*	4 *carrots*
3 *turnips*	6 *small onions*
1 *stick celery*	*water*
2 *leeks*	*pepper*

Order the meat at least one week before it is needed and ask the butcher to put it in brine. Before preparing the meat for the oven, put it to soak in water for at least six hours. Dry the meat and put it in a deep earthenware stewpot. Add the vegetables cut into pieces, season with pepper and pour in enough water barely to cover the meat. Cook in a moderate oven for two or three hours or until the meat is tender. Remove to a hot serving-dish, surround the meat with the vegetables and serve with boiled potatoes.

Stewed Steak

2 *lb. shoulder steak*	*water*
1 *Spanish onion*	*salt and pepper*
flour	

Cut the meat into two inch cubes and place in a deep earthenware oven dish. Add the sliced onion and season with salt and pepper. Barely cover with water, put on a lid and place in a hot oven. Reduce the heat of the oven after twenty minutes and cook slowly for at least two hours until the meat is done. Thicken the gravy by the addition of a little flour and water. The appearance of this dish is improved by stirring in a little gravy browning, but some purists raise their eyebrows in horror at the thought.

Steak and Cowheel Pie

2 *lb. shoulder steak*   *shortcrust pastry (p.* 167)
1 *small cowheel*   *salt and pepper*

Trim the steak and cut into small serving pieces. Cut the cowheel into similar portions and put together with the steak in a stew jar. Cover with water, season with salt and pepper and stew slowly in a moderate oven for two hours. Allow to cool and remove all the bones from the cowheel before transferring to a pie dish and putting on the pie crust. If the dish is not full use a pie funnel. Cook in a hot oven for thirty or forty minutes until the crust is golden. Serve with boiled potatoes.

Steak and Cowheel Pie with a Suet Crust

1½ *lb. shoulder steak*   *water*
1 *small cowheel*   *salt and pepper*
1 *small onion*   *suet crust (p.* 92)

Cut the cowheel and the meat into pieces and put them into a pan together with the onion cut into four pieces. Cover with water, season with salt and pepper, bring to the boil and simmer for about two hours until the meat is cooked. When cool enough to handle, remove all the bones and put the meat and the liquid into a pie dish. Cover with a suet crust and bake for about forty minutes in a moderate oven until the crust is well browned. Serve with boiled potatoes.

Suet Crust

> 6 *oz. flour*   *milk*
> 3 *oz. chopped suet*   *salt and pepper*
> 1 *teaspoon baking powder*

Mix the flour and suet together and add the baking powder, salt and pepper and enough milk to make a fairly firm dough. Roll out the dough very lightly and put it on the pie dish. This suet crust may also be used for a steak and kidney pie.

Steak and Kidney Pie

> 1½ *lb. stewing steak*   1 *bay leaf*
> 1 *veal kidney*   4 *oz. shortcrust pastry (p.*
> *salt and pepper*   167)
> *flour*

Cut the steak into pieces about one inch square, trim the kidney of all fat and skin it carefully. If the kidney has a strong flavour scald with boiling water before cutting it into small pieces. Lightly flour and season the meat and put it into a deep oven dish. Cover with water, put in the bay leaf, and stew gently in a moderate oven for about one hour and a half when the meat should be tender. Remove from the oven and allow to cool before putting on the pie crust. Return to a hot oven and bake for about half an hour until the crust is golden.

Steak and Kidney Plate Pie

> 1½ *lb. stewing steak*   *salt and pepper*
> 1 *small veal kidney*   *shortcrust pastry (p.* 167)
> *flour*

Trim the steak and the kidney and cut into small pieces. Dip each piece in seasoned flour and put to stew gently barely covered with water while the pie crust is being prepared. Line a buttered pie-plate with thinly rolled pastry, put in the slightly cooled meat, cover with a thin layer of pastry, make two slits in the top and bake in a hot oven for half an hour.

This pie is equally good eaten hot or cold.

Steak and Kidney Pudding

Ruth Pinch, a character in *Martin Chuzzlewit* by Charles Dickens, used six ounces of butter instead of suet for her pudding crust and moistened it with four egg yolks beaten with a little water, but otherwise her recipe is the same as Eliza Acton's (*Modern Cookery for Private Families*, 1845). I favour Miss Acton's recipe myself but add kidney and cannot afford the oysters.

6 *oz. suet crust* (*p.* 92)	1 *veal kidney*
1½ *lb. round steak*	*salt and pepper*

Line a buttered pudding basin with thinly rolled suet crust, leaving enough for the top. Trim the meat and the kidney and cut them into small pieces. Fill the pudding basin with the meat, seasoning each layer with salt and pepper, and add enough water to cover the meat. Damp the edge of the crust, put on the lid and turn in the edges so that the gravy does not escape during cooking. Cover with buttered greaseproof paper or foil and tie down with a pudding cloth. Place the pudding in a pan half full of boiling water, add a tablespoon of vinegar to the water and boil for three hours, keeping the water at the same level.

Oxtail with Butter Beans

1 *or* 2 *oxtails*	1½ *teacups butter beans*
6 *shallots*	*salt and pepper*
4 *carrots*	*water*

Trim the tails of any surplus fat and joint them carefully. Put them in an earthenware stew jar with the shallots, sliced carrots and beans. Season with salt and pepper, cover with water, put on the lid of the stew jar and place in a moderate oven. Cook slowly for at least four hours until the meat is tender and will leave the bone. It may be necessary to add a little hot water as the beans swell, in which case adjust the seasoning.

Oxtail Mould

1 *large or 2 small oxtails*	*a faggot of herbs*
1 *onion*	*pepper and salt*
4 *cloves*	*water*
1 *wineglass of red wine*	*2 hard-boiled eggs*

Trim the fat off the oxtails and cut them into pieces at the joints. Put the meat in a stew pan with the onion cut into quarters and stuck with cloves, the wine and herbs, and season with pepper and salt. Cover with water and stew for at least four hours until the meat leaves the bones. When cool enough to handle, take all the meat off the bones and put it into a plain mould lined with sliced hard-boiled eggs (a cake tin will do admirably). Strain in as much of the liquor as the mould will take and leave to go cold. Turn out to serve on a bed of lettuce and send to table with a salad.

Oxtail Stew

1 *or 2 oxtails*	*salt and pepper*
1 *onion*	*water*

Trim the oxtails of some of the fat and carefully divide into pieces at the joints. Put the meat into an earthenware stew jar with a lid. Add the sliced onion, season with salt and pepper and cover with water. Stew in a moderate oven for at least three or four hours when the meat should fall easily from the bones and be ready to serve. Wrap a white napkin round the stew jar and serve with potatoes baked in their skins.

Ox Tongue

Ox tongues can usually be bought from the butcher already brined but if you can only obtain an unsalted one, you can brine it at home or cook it unsalted, though I think it looks and tastes better brined. Prepare the brine bath as follows:

1 *lb. kitchen salt*	*enough water to cover the*
¾ *oz. saltpetre*	*tongue completely*
6 *oz. brown sugar*	

This brine may also be used for beef (see Boiled Beef, p. 96). Dissolve the ingredients in the measured water and boil for twenty minutes. Skim and allow to cool. Put the tongue in a deep earthenware dish and cover with the brine. Ten days should do nicely. If the tongue is not completely immersed in the brine, it must be turned each day. It should be kept in a cold larder or a refrigerator.

ox tongue	1 *celery stalk*
6 *peppercorns*	*faggot of herbs*
2 *medium-sized onions*	*water*
2 *carrots*	*salt (if unbrined)*

When the tongue is ready to cook, remove it from the brine and immerse it in cold water for one hour. Have ready a large pan with enough cold water to cover the tongue and add the peppercorns, onions, carrots, celery and a faggot of herbs. Bring slowly to the boil, skim as necessary and simmer gently about four hours. If the tongue is fresh, add some salt to the water. When the tongue is cooked, allow it to cool in the liquid until cool enough to handle. Remove all the bones and fat from the root of the tongue and peel off the skin. This is a messy job and as the skin comes away more easily if the tongue

95

is hot, it is as well to have a bowl of cold water at hand to dip your hands in from time to time. The tongue is now ready to serve hot. Place on a large dish and serve with spinach, mashed or boiled potatoes and either Cumberland or parsley sauce (see Chapter 2).

If the tongue is to be eaten cold, shape it into a round and fit it into a round cake tin pressing it well down. Add some of the liquid in which the tongue was boiled and this will jellify when cold. Press the meat into the tin with a plate and weight it down and leave for twenty-four hours before turning it out to serve.

Boiled Beef

Use the same method for brining the beef as given for ox tongue (p. 95) if the butcher has not already done it for you. Many country butchers have tongue and joints of beef in brine all the time. Silverside, brisket, aitchbone and topside are all suitable joints. Salted brisket is usually used for cold pressed beef but any of the others mentioned are good to use for boiled beef and dumplings.

4–5 *lb. beef joint (see above)*	3 *or* 4 *cloves*
1 *bay leaf*	5 *or* 6 *small onions*
parsley	5 *or* 6 *carrots*
thyme	2 *turnips*
6 *peppercorns*	*suet dumplings (p.* 184)
1 *medium-size onion*	

Put the brined joint in a pan with enough unsalted water to cover it. Bring slowly to the boil and skim as necessary. Add the bay leaf, a few parsley stalks and a sprig of thyme tied together, the peppercorns, one medium-size onion stuck with three or four cloves, the small onions, the carrots sliced into quarters lengthwise and two turnips cut into quarters. Simmer for one and a half hours then remove the onion and the herbs. Put in the prepared vegetables and simmer for another hour or until both the meat and vegetables are just tender. Add dumplings and cook for twenty minutes with the pan lid on. Arrange on a large dish with the vegetables and dumplings surrounding the meat and serve with boiled potatoes and caper sauce (p. 19).

Meat Loaf

1 *lb. freshly minced raw beef*
4 *oz. fat salt pork (minced)*
1 *pint fresh breadcrumbs*
2 *oz. chopped onion*
1 *teaspoon mixed herbs*
   (*chives, chervil, fennel and*
   tarragon)
1 *tablespoon Worcestershire*
   sauce

1 *teaspoon mushroom catsup*
1 *teaspoon celery salt*
1 *teaspoon salt*
pepper
1 *tablespoon olive oil*
1 *tablespoon cold water*
2 *eggs*

Mix all the ingredients together and knead well with the hands. Bind with the beaten eggs and form into a roll. If preferred, the mixture may be pressed into an oiled loaf tin. Leave in a cold larder or refrigerator for at least one hour, then take out the mixture and place in a well-greased baking-dish and cook in a moderate oven for at least one hour. Serve with a rich tomato sauce (p. 31). The meat loaf may equally well be cooked in the sauce.

Potted Beef

2 *lb. shin beef*
water
4 *oz. butter*

pounded mace
salt and pepper

Cut the meat into very small pieces and remove as much fat as possible. It may then be put into a stew jar, a double boiler or a pressure cooker. Barely cover the meat with water, season with salt, a pinch of mace and freshly ground black pepper and cook until the meat is quite tender. This will take anything from one to four hours according to the method of cooking.

When the meat has cooked, put it through the mincer, then pound it in a mortar adding the gravy run from the meat and two ounces of butter. Pot and when cold cover with melted butter to keep.

Beef Tea

| 1 *lb. lean shin beef* | $\frac{1}{2}$ *teaspoon salt* |
| 1 *pint water* | |

An old fashioned but delectable recipe for invalids, it is still a cheap way of providing nourishment and delicious potted beef. Cut one pound of lean shin beef into small pieces and put them into a double boiler or a stoneware pot if you have one. Add a pint of cold water and cook very slowly indeed for at least four hours on a low heat or overnight in a simmering oven if using a stoneware pot. Halfway through the cooking add half a teaspoon of salt. When all the nutritious juices have been extracted from the beef, strain and remove any particles of fat. The stoneware pot lid should be sealed.

The beef may be pounded well, seasoned and potted. Cover the pot with clarified butter.

Tripe and Onions

Tripe and onions is a North Country dish, and it is here that the best dressed tripe is found. In the south of England it is all too often so bleached as to be quite tasteless.

Most cookery books call for hours of stewing, but this is quite unnecessary when using dressed tripe. Indeed, in Lancashire, tripe is frequently eaten uncooked, just as it comes from the tripe shop, with a good dash of malt vinegar, salt and pepper.

1 *large Spanish onion*	1 *pint milk*
2 *lb. thick seam tripe*	2 *tablespoons flour*
2 *oz. butter*	*salt and pepper*

Chop the onion roughly, cover with water and simmer gently while the tripe is being cut into serving portions. Put the pieces of tripe into the pan with the onion, season with salt and pepper and stew gently for half an hour to allow the tripe to absorb the flavour of the onion. Add the milk and butter and bring to the boil. Adjust the seasoning. Mix the flour with a little milk and stir into the contents of the pan with an extra knob of butter. Serve with mashed potatoes.

LAMB

Roast Lamb

Although with modern methods of refrigeration and the availability of imported meat, we can have lamb, frozen peas and tinned new potatoes all the year round, they cannot compare with young Southdown or Welsh lamb in the spring when the first Jersey potatoes and the first garden peas are picked. Alas, this is a rare delicacy nowadays, particularly for those who live in towns. The meat on a shoulder is succulent and sweeter than on a leg with less bone and fat and, therefore, a better buy. New Zealand lamb can be very good providing a joint with very little fat on it is available.

shoulder or *leg lamb*	*juice of* 1 *lemon*
salt and black pepper	*rosemary* or *garlic* (*if liked*)
fat or *olive oil*	

Remove any thick pieces of fat and put them in the roasting tin to cook with the lamb. Rub the outside of the joint with kitchen salt, black pepper and olive oil and squeeze the juice of a small lemon over the meat. A sprig or two of rosemary or a few slivers of garlic (not both) inserted under the skin enhances the flavour of the meat.

Put the meat into a hot oven and when sizzling noises are heard then it is time to lower the heat to moderate and cook for one or one and a half hours when the joint should be ready for eating. Timing depends rather on the size of the joint and also whether you like lamb well done or slightly pink near the bone. It may be tested by inserting a fine skewer into the meat. If a pink fluid runs out then leave for another ten minutes in a cooling oven. Slow cooking is advisable for lamb so that it may be well cooked and avoid shrinkage.

Crown Roast of Lamb

A crown roast of lamb is fashioned from the best end of neck, twelve to sixteen cutlets of which are required to form the crown. This is definitely a party dish and a good butcher will know how to prepare a crown roast for you. In case he doesn't, the following directions will help if you have to tell him how it is done.

Usually weighing between six and seven pounds, the ribs are separated at the backbone but left together so that when serving, the knife goes down between each one or two of the cutlets and the section is lifted out and served with some of the stuffing which may vary according to taste, but is usually a mixture of equal parts of chopped lamb trimmings and pork sausage meat highly flavoured and spiced. When ordering your own crown roast ask the butcher to wrap pieces of salt pork around the ends of each 'frenched' rib to prevent charring during roasting.

crown roast (12 *to* 16 *cutlets*)	3 *shallots*
cooking oil	2 *carrots*
faggot of herbs (*see below*)	1 *stick celery*
2 *cloves*	

To cook a crown roast, first wipe it with a damp cloth then rub in some cooking oil. If the butcher has not wrapped the rib ends with strips of salt pork, cover each one with a piece of foil to prevent burning. Place a faggot of herbs, composed of one large bay leaf tied together with a small bunch of parsley and some celery tops and a sprig of thyme, in the pan with two whole cloves, the shallots, carrots and celery all coarsely chopped. Sear the roast over a bright flame for fifteen or twenty minutes, basting frequently with the vegetables and fat dripping from the lamb. When well browned transfer to a moderate oven first pouring half a cup of boiling water into the roasting-tin with the vegetables. Put the stuffing in the centre of the roast and season with salt and black pepper. Cook for one and a half to two hours according to the weight of meat and baste frequently to prevent the meat from drying up.

If stuffing is not liked, a cup placed in the centre of the roast will keep the crown in good shape. When ready to serve remove the cup, transfer the roast to a hot serving-dish and fill the centre with creamed mushrooms (p. 147) or creamed sweetbreads (pp. 105 and 114). Make the gravy by swilling some vegetable water round the roasting-tin, scraping up the browned bits with a wooden spoon and serve in a gravy-boat. A crown roast is usually served with mint sauce or jelly (pp. 27 and 221), buttered brussels sprouts and dry baked potatoes. Cranberry sauce or quince jelly are even better.

Stuffed Breast of Lamb

Ask the butcher to bone the breasts for you and remove any surplus fat. Prepare a sage and onion stuffing and put some in the centre of each breast. Roll and secure the breasts, but not too tightly. Wrap each one in aluminium foil and enclose firmly. Place them in a moderate oven and cook for one and a half to two hours. If the breasts have not browned nicely, put them back in the oven without the foil but take care they do not dry up or the meat will be tough and stringy instead of tender and succulent. They are equally good eaten hot or cold.

Breast of veal may be treated the same way in which case a forcemeat stuffing should be used instead of sage and onion (see Stuffings).

Hot Pot

Hot pot is originally a Lancashire dish and in the days when oysters were less of a luxury than they are today, they were often put into a hot pot instead of pigs' tails.

1 *lb. best end of neck of lamb*	1 *lb. onions*
1 *lb. shoulder steak*	3 *lb. potatoes*
2 *pigs' tails*	*salt and pepper*
1 *pig's foot*	*water*

Cut the steak into one-inch squares, the lamb and the pig's foot as near the same size as possible, allowing for the boning. Slice the pigs' tails into pieces, put all together into a hot-pot dish or large stew jar and season well with salt and pepper. Add the sliced onions and cover with water. Put a lid on the pot and stew for at least two hours in a moderate oven. This can be done the day before the hot pot is to be eaten. While still warm, remove as many bones as possible. Cut most of the potatoes into small pieces, stir them into the meat and adjust the seasoning. Replace the lid and put back into the oven until the potatoes are nearly cooked. Have ready some thinly sliced large potatoes and arrange them on top of the hot pot. Dust with a little seasoned flour and put back in the oven until the potatoes are browned and crisp.

Wrap a white napkin round the dish and serve with pickled red cabbage or pickled onions.

Irish Stew

1½ lb. neck of mutton or   2 large onions
    lamb   salt and pepper
2 lb. potatoes   ¾ pint water

Breast of mutton or lamb is equally good for this dish but may be too fat for some tastes.

Trim the meat of some of the fat and cut into pieces. Peel and slice the potatoes and onions. Put a layer of potatoes at the bottom of a stew pan or jar followed by a layer of meat and onions and continue to fill the pan or jar, seasoning each layer with salt and pepper and finishing with a generous layer of potatoes. Pour in the water and stew very gently for two hours, keeping the lid tightly closed. Shake the pan occasionally to prevent the stew from burning; stirring with a spoon might make the potatoes mushy.

Serve with sliced boiled beetroot in vinegar, pickled onions or pickled red cabbage.

Lamb Pie

3 lb. baby lamb   salt and pepper
1½ lb. small new potatoes   shortcrust pastry (p. 167)
mint

This dish can only be made in the spring during the short season of new potatoes and very young lamb. It should be made in a deep glazed earthenware hot-pot dish.

Cut the lamb into serving pieces and put into the dish. Season with salt and pepper, cover with water and place in a moderate oven for about one and a half hours or until the meat is nearly done. Next put in the scraped potatoes and a few sprigs of mint. Put on the pie crust and bake in a hot oven for twenty to thirty minutes until the crust is crisp and golden.

103

Lamb Ragout (1)

A spring and early summer favourite when the lamb is young and the first garden peas are ready. Nowadays the season is lengthened by the availability of imported meat and frozen peas, but it cannot be so good as when made with baby lamb and fresh young vegetables.

3 *lb. best end neck of lamb*	*salt and pepper*
1 *medium-size onion*	*sugar*
1 *lb. young carrots*	*fresh mint*
1 *lb. shelled garden peas*	*water*

Trim and cut the meat into manageable pieces, put them into a saucepan and cover with water. Add the finely sliced onion and the carrots. Leave them whole if they are small, if not slice them. Bring slowly to the boil, skim carefully and simmer gently for one hour. Add the peas and a bunch of fresh mint, season with salt, pepper and sugar to taste, and cook gently until the peas are ready. Remove the mint before serving with boiled new potatoes.

Lamb Ragout (2)

A winter version of the preceding recipe. For this, the meat does not need to be so young and the amount of onion is increased.

3 *lb. neck end of lamb*	4 *oz. pearl barley*
3 *onions*	*salt and pepper*
1 *lb. carrots*	*water*

Cut up the meat, cover with water and bring to the boil. Add the finely sliced onions and carrots, and throw in the pearl barley. Season to taste and simmer gently for two hours or until the meat is cooked and the barley soft. Serve with boiled or jacket potatoes and freshly boiled or pickled beetroot.

Lamb Sweetbreads

1 *lb. sweetbreads*	2 *tablespoons flour*
1 *oz. butter*	*salt and pepper*
¾ *pint white stock*	1 *teaspoon lemon juice*

Let the sweetbreads lie in warm water for about one hour then wipe them dry and dust them with flour. Heat the butter and sauté the sweetbreads in it for five minutes. Cover them with the hot stock, season and simmer gently for thirty minutes. Mix one tablespoon of flour with a little cold water until smooth and add to the broth. Stir in the lemon juice, pour over the sweetbreads, and cook for ten minutes more. Serve very hot, garnished with slices of lemon.

PORK

Roast Pork

A cut off the leg, spare rib or loin are all good for roasting though many prefer to have the loin in chop form. Pork can be tough and rather indigestible unless it is young. Personally, I never buy pork from which the rind has been cut because, while this is sometimes done to remove some of the fat, particularly on the loin, it is difficult to tell the age of the meat without it unless you trust your butcher. Young pork has a soft skin which becomes harder and tough with age. Suckling pig is best of all but very expensive and hard to come by unless you know a breeder who will let you have one.

The skin is usually scored by the butcher and a loin cut chined to make for easier carving. This can be done at home but you will need a very sharp pointed knife and a hatchet.

leg, spare rib or loin of pork   *salt and pepper*
cooking oil or *pork dripping*

Rub the oil or dripping all over the outside of the meat and especially where the rind has been scored. Next rub salt and pepper into the rind only to ensure good crackling. Put the joint in a moderately hot oven and baste from time to time allowing thirty minutes to the pound. If cooked in a self-baster or under foil, remove for the last half hour so that the crackling becomes really crisp. Crackling, of course, is loved by some and hated by others. Make sure the pork is really cooked through before serving.

The usual accompaniments for roast pork are sage and onion stuffing (p. 37; stuff the meat if it has been boned, otherwise cook the stuffing separately in a fireproof dish), apple sauce (p. 17) and roast potatoes.

Loin of Pork with Quince

loin of pork	*olive oil*
6 *quinces*	*salt and pepper*
2 *oz. sugar*	

Choose young pork, not too fat, and ask your butcher to score the skin for you. Allow one quince for each person. Peel and slice the fruit, sprinkle them with sugar and leave them for half an hour. Rub the meat all over with olive oil, salt and pepper, particularly the scored skin and put into a roasting-pan with the quince arranged round the meat. Cover with foil and place in a hot oven. Reduce the heat after twenty minutes and baste frequently until the meat is thoroughly cooked (allow thirty minutes to the pound) and the skin blistered and crackling. Leave the foil off for the last half hour of cooking.

Serve with a sage and onion stuffing (p. 37) baked separately in a flat dish and dry baked potatoes (p. 153).

Pork Pestel (Hock)

A dish both filling and satisfying on a cold winter's day. Not only is it cheap and nourishing but also very delicious. In some parts of the country a pork hock is known as a pestel but in case your butcher hasn't heard of it under this name, ask him to give you a meaty hock.

1 *pork pestel*	*salt and pepper*
3 *leeks*	*water*
½ *lb. marrowfat peas*	*bicarbonate of soda*
1 *lb. carrots*	*suet dumplings (p. 184)*

Wash the pestel, put it in a large pan, cover with water and bring to the boil. Skim and reduce the heat. Cut the leeks into two-inch lengths using all the white part and some of the green. Slice the carrots and rinse the peas which have been soaked overnight in boiling water and a pinch of bicarbonate of soda. Add the vegetables to the meat and simmer gently over a low fire for two or three hours according to the size of the pestel.

Have ready some suet dumplings and when the meat seems nearly cooked arrange them in the pan and cook with the lid on until they are light and fluffy (about twenty minutes). Remove the meat from the pan on to a warmed serving-dish, arrange the dumplings around it with any of the vegetables which have not disintegrated, and serve with floury boiled potatoes.

The broth may be served as a first course and is improved by the addition of a little malt vinegar. This should be added at table being a matter of individual taste.

Pork Pie

1 *lb. lean pork*	*pepper and salt*
1 *sour apple*	1 *lb. raised pie crust (p. 166)*
1 *teaspoon sugar*	*egg yolk*
a pinch of powdered cloves	*jellied stock (p. 57)*

Cut the meat into small pieces. Peel, core and slice the apple finely and mix with the meat, together with the sugar, cloves and seasoning. Sprinkle with one tablespoon water. Wash any bones, place them in a pan, barely cover with water and simmer gently to make stock for the pie. Make the raised pie crust according to the recipe given on page 166. Cut off about a quarter for the top of the pie and leave in a warm place until needed. With the remainder, line a raised pie mould or shape with the hands round a jar to help keep the pie upright. Fill the pie with the meat and roll out the pastry for the lid. Pinch the edges close together, first wetting them with water, trim and decorate with cuts of pastry and make a hole in the centre of the lid to allow the steam to escape. Brush the top with egg yolk and if a mould is not being used, tie two or three sheets of greaseproof paper round the pie to keep it in shape. Bake in a moderately hot oven (400° F) for about an hour, then reduce the oven heat to 350° F and cook until the meat seems tender when tested with a skewer. If the top is getting too brown, lay a piece of greaseproof paper over it. Remove the pie from the oven when done and fill the pie with hot well-seasoned stock.

Collared Head (Brawn)

½ *pig's head*	1 *medium-size onion*
6 *peppercorns*	*water*
1 *bay leaf*	*salt and pepper*

Cut up the head and put the meat into a pan with the pepper-corns, bay leaf and the onion left whole. Barely cover with water and season with salt and pepper. Simmer gently for two hours, skimming when necessary. When the meat seems to be falling from the bones remove from the fire and leave in the liquor until cool enough to handle. Take the meat from the bones, chop it into small pieces and put it into a wetted mould. Pour in enough liquor to cover the meat and leave to set.

Ham

If you have to boil a whole ham, the following times will be useful:

12 lb. ham	$3\frac{1}{2}$ hours
14 lb. ham	$3\frac{3}{4}$ hours
16 lb. ham	4 hours

In each case leave for thirty minutes in the stock if it is to be eaten hot, and let it go cold in the stock if the ham is to be eaten cold.

Nowadays both bacon and ham joints are to be found in the market. If the meat is red it is likely to be salty and should be soaked for some hours in cold water before cooking, particularly if it is to be baked in the oven.

Ham, Beans and Onion

2 *lb. thick sliced gammon*   1 *tablespoon beef dripping*
2 *large onions*   *pepper*
4 *oz. boiled haricot beans*

Trim the rind and fat from the ham. Peel and chop the onions and fry them lightly in the beef dripping until the onions are soft. Cut the ham rind into inch long pieces and add to the onions. Add the beans, with a good grind of pepper, cover and cook slowly stirring from time to time. Meanwhile, grill the ham slices and serve the hot beans separately.

Baked Ham (1)

A corner or cushion of ham is most suitable for cooking in the following manner. Soak well in cold water.

Make a soft flour and water dough and roll out large enough to enfold the ham completely. Seal the dough carefully, put it into a roasting-tin and place in a moderate oven for one or two hours according to the size of the piece of ham (twenty-five to thirty minutes per pound). Insert a skewer to see if the ham is cooked, crack open the dough shell and serve the ham hot or cold.

Baked Ham (2)

Soak well, then closely stick the top of a ham roast with cloves, sprinkle with brown sugar and put into a baking-dish. Add one pint of cider and cover with foil. Bake in a moderate oven until the meat is tender (twenty-five to thirty minutes per pound). Delicious served hot with new potatoes, young broad beans smothered in parsley sauce or cold with pickled peaches (p. 222).

Boiled Bacon and Broad Beans

Choose a piece of streaky bacon, not less than two pounds in weight. Put it into a pan, barely cover with cold water, and bring to the boil slowly. Simmer for ten minutes then remove the pan from the fire and let the bacon stand in the water in which it has cooked for ten minutes more. Serve hot with broad beans, parsley sauce and new potatoes, or cold with a salad.

Sausages

There are many branded sausages on the market today but very few of them are as good as those made by a butcher who takes pride in the quality of his meat and makes his own sausages, for these usually contain a good deal more meat and less bread and fat which reduces their size when cooked.

Sausages should be grilled or cooked in the top of a hot oven rather than fried, and under no circumstances should fat be added to the pan they are cooked in. Separate the sausages and prick each one two or three times with a fork to allow the air under the skins to escape and prevent the sausages from bursting. Turn them once or twice while cooking to ensure even cooking and browning.

Traditional accompaniment—mashed potatoes (p. 153).

VEAL

Veal, Roast

In England today, veal is not easy to find outside London where it is a very expensive import, mainly from Holland. In my opinion, veal is not for roasting unless it be very young and the best cut for roasting is the loin, boned, or the top part of the leg: between three and four pounds is a reasonable joint.

The method of cooking is much the same as other roasts but because it is a naturally dry meat, it should be rubbed over with butter, beef dripping or olive oil, then salt and pepper.

Have the oven very hot and put the joint in a roasting-tin with some beef dripping. It should be very well cooked and basted several times while cooking. Allow at least twenty minutes to the pound.

A little lemon juice squeezed over the joint and a sprig or two of rosemary in the pan is an improvement.

Veal, Stuffed

For two pounds of shoulder veal the following makes a very good stuffing:

4 *oz. breadcrumbs*	2 *garlic cloves crushed*
2 *lemons*	2 *tablespoons olive oil*
1 *teaspoon thyme*	1 *egg*
1 *teaspoon sweet basil*	*salt and pepper*
1 *teaspoon finely chopped*	1 *pint stock*
parsley	

Put the breadcrumbs into a bowl and add the grated rind of both lemons, the finely chopped herbs (fresh if possible), one crushed garlic clove, and the juice of one lemon. Mix well together and moisten with the egg. If the meat is thick, make a slit to insert the stuffing; otherwise, flatten the meat out and rub a crushed garlic clove and some salt and pepper over the inside of the meat. Place the stuffing on the meat and roll and tie carefully into shape. Put the olive oil in the bottom of a heavy casserole and heat before putting in the meat. Cook on top of the stove for some minutes, turning the meat to brown all over then transfer the casserole to a hot oven. When the meat is sizzling, pour over the juice of the other lemon. Add one pint of white stock, cover the casserole and cook in a slow oven for about two hours. Cut into slices to serve with jacket potatoes and a green salad.

Calf's Head

calf's head	*dash of vinegar*
faggot of herbs	*salt and black pepper*
bay leaf	*water*

If asked and given time, your butcher will remove the eyes and generally prepare the head for cooking. He will remove the brains and tongue though some cooks prefer to leave the tongue in the head.

Soak the head in salted water for one hour, then put into a large pan with enough cold water to cover the head. Add a faggot of herbs, bay leaf and a dash of vinegar, and season with salt and black pepper. Bring to boiling point and skim off any scum rising to the surface. Simmer gently until the meat is falling from the bones, which should take about two hours, or less if using a pressure cooker.

Let the head cool in the water and when cool enough to handle, remove the bones, skin the tongue and cut into slices. Cut the meat into pieces about two inches square, reheat and serve with boiled potatoes and a sharp sauce such as caper sauce, Chelford sauce or a vinegar and oil dressing, adding a tablespoon of chopped parsley (see Chapter 2). The brains may be cooked with the head or saved for another dish.

Calf's head is very good pressed and served cold and the liquor is a very good basis for soup.

Veal Kidneys with Red Wine

3 *veal kidneys*	1 *glass red wine*
flour	*salt and pepper*
2 *oz. butter*	1 *glass sherry* or *marsala*

Choose the smallest kidneys you can find unless you like the rather strong flavour of large ones, which should be scalded in boiling water for a few minutes before using.

Trim the kidneys and cut them into small pieces about the size of a five pence piece. Flour them well and put them into a pan in which you have melted two ounces of butter. Toss them for a minute or two in the foaming butter then add the red wine. Season with salt and pepper, cover the pan and let them stew until tender. Twenty minutes should be enough.

Just before serving add a small glass of sherry or marsala and serve with creamed potatoes.

Veal and Ham Pie

1 *knuckle of veal sawn into three pieces*	1 *tablespoon mixed herbs*
	a pinch of summer savory
1 *lb. stewing veal*	1 *onion quartered*
1 *teaspoon of lemon juice*	*pepper*
1 *lb. unsmoked ham*	3 *hard-boiled eggs*
2 *bay leaves*	*shortcrust pastry (p.* 167)

Cover the veal bones with water and lemon juice and stew them until they are soft. Cut the ham and veal into small squares and put into an earthenware stew jar with the herbs and onion, and season with black pepper. Cover with the liquor from the veal bones and cook until the meat is tender. Taste for seasoning as it may be necessary to add salt. Arrange the meat in a pie dish with the hard-boiled eggs cut in halves and remove the bay leaves and onion. Pour in the liquor and cover with a pie crust. If the dish is not full use a pie funnel or an inverted egg cup. Crimp the edges of the pastry with a fork, make two slashes in the top of the pie and brush the top with milk. Place in a hot oven for twenty to thirty minutes or until the pie crust is cooked. Serve hot or cold.

Veal Sweetbreads

3 *veal sweetbreads*	1 *oz. butter*
4 *oz. mushrooms*	1 *oz. flour*
½ *pint white stock*	½ *pint cream*
1 *teaspoon lemon juice*	*salt and pepper*

Soak the sweetbreads in warm water for one hour, then bring them to the boil and simmer for ten minutes. Remove from the fire and put them into cold water for a few minutes. Cut the sweetbreads into pieces, slice the mushrooms, and put them into a stew pan. Cover with seasoned stock, add the lemon juice and simmer for half an hour. Lift the sweetbreads out of the pan, put them on a serving-dish and keep them warm while making the sauce. Thicken the stock with the butter and flour, add the cream and heat, stirring constantly to keep the sauce smooth. Do not let it boil but when quite hot pour over the sweetbreads and serve.

MISCELLANEOUS

Brains

Although calves' brains are considered to be the best, they are difficult to obtain in England today owing to the scarcity of veal. Sheep or lambs' brains are very good and any of the following recipes will serve.

One and a half pounds should serve six people. Soak the brains for several hours in cold water, changing the water from time to time. This is done to clean the brains of blood. Remove any ligaments, veins and skin and put the brains in warm water to remove any final traces of blood.

Prepare a court bouillon with two pints of water, one teaspoon of salt, a small onion stuck with three or four cloves, two tablespoons of wine vinegar, or one of vinegar and the other lemon juice, a faggot of herbs and six peppercorns. Bring to the boil and simmer for twenty minutes and allow it to cool. When cool, put in the brains and bring them slowly to the boil and simmer for half an hour. The brains are now ready to serve in several ways:

(1) They may be chopped coarsely and added to a rich white sauce (p. 32) and served with mashed potatoes, or used to fill vol-au-vent cases.

(2) They may be sliced and fried in butter and served with a

sauce of melted butter containing a pinch of salt, a squeeze of lemon juice and a good sprinkling of freshly ground black pepper.

(3) Slice and marinate the brains in the juice of one lemon, a handful of chopped parsley, one tablespoon of olive oil, salt and pepper. Leave the brains for two hours at least in the marinade then dip them in breadcrumbs or flour and fry quickly in very hot oil. Drain on kitchen paper and serve with leaf spinach and creamy mashed potatoes.

Alternatively, blanch the brains in water with a little salt, lemon juice or vinegar. Poach gently, for ten minutes at most, then place them in a casserole. Pour caper sauce (p. 20) over them and re-heat in the oven.

Black butter sauce with or without the addition of capers is excellent with poached and coarsely chopped brains. Serve brains with small boiled potatoes.

Cottage Pie

In some parts of the country this dish is known as Shepherd's pie but it is the same dish. It was traditionally made from the left-over meat from the Sunday joint, which in my view is better eaten cold.

Made from freshly minced meat and creamy mashed potatoes it is quite delicious.

2 *lb. minced meat*	1 *tablespoon tomato paste*
1 *Spanish* or 2 *smaller onions*	4 *oz. butter*
1 *teacup water*	2 *lb. potatoes*
1 *tablespoon olive oil*	*salt and pepper*
1 *tablespoon chopped parsley*	*milk*

If you are buying the meat from your butcher ready minced, make sure it has been through the mincer twice as otherwise the mince tends to be lumpy when cooked.

Grate the onions and put them in a pan with a teacupful

of water. Let them simmer until soft then add the mince, olive oil, tomato paste, parsley and two ounces of butter. Season well with salt and freshly ground black pepper. Constant stirring is necessary to amalgamate all the ingredients and to prevent burning. When the meat has changed colour and is partly cooked, put into a well-buttered ovenproof dish and cover with mashed potatoes into which have been stirred the rest of the butter and enough milk to make the potatoes creamy but not runny. Score the top with a fork or form it into a whirl, and cook in a moderate oven for an hour or until the top is nicely browned.

Serve with pickled onions or pickled red cabbage (see Chapter 8).

Liver and Onions

2 *lb. liver*	1 *teacup cooking oil*
2 *large Spanish onions*	1½ *oz. butter*
flour	

If the liver is no longer very young, cut it into thin slices and lay them in hot milk for three minutes. Pour away the milk and the liver is ready for cooking, tender and improved in flavour.

Slice the onions and dredge them with flour. Heat one teacup of oil in a frying-pan and when very hot, put in the sliced onions. Fry them quickly until crisp and golden, then take them off the fire and put them to drain on kitchen paper. Keep them warm while the liver is being cooked. Any oil left in the pan after frying the onions may be used, or if preferred, the liver may be fried in butter.

Melt one and a half ounces of butter in a clean frying-pan and when very hot but not brown, put in the thinly cut slices of liver. They will take about five minutes to cook. When they are ready, arrange them on a hot serving-dish with the onions and serve at once.

8. Poultry and Game

Chicken

At one time chicken was a luxury and eaten only on special occasions or as a change from the Sunday roast. With the modern methods of production the price of a chicken today is comparable with meat and sometimes even cheaper, so more variety in cooking is called for than the inevitable roast chicken. Nevertheless, a good roast chicken takes some beating, especially for those with a source of supply other than the foreign frozen birds which nowadays flood the supermarkets. These birds have little flavour and need to be cooked with wine, onions or herbs to give them character.

When choosing a chicken, or any other poultry, wiggle the breast bone. If it is soft and flexible, it means the bird is young. It has been known for a poulterer to break the breastbone so that it seems flexible to the inexpert shopper, but it should also be soft gristle and this cannot be simulated. Corn-fed chickens have a yellow flesh and are preferred by some cooks. For my taste a chicken should be plump and white-fleshed, and a short stocky bird is preferable to a long rangy one. If you have many to feed, ask for a capon, which is a rooster gelded to improve the flesh and increase the growth. A capon usually weighs between six and eight pounds.

Roast Chicken

young chicken or *capon*   1 *small onion*

118

oil or *butter*   6 *slices streaky bacon*
salt and pepper

Check that the bird has been cleaned thoroughly and if necessary wipe it over with a damp cloth, but on no account rinse
the bird with water or you will lose the delicate flavour of the
chicken. Put a small peeled onion inside the bird and rub the
breast with oil or butter, salt and pepper. Put a lump of butter
in each of the leg joints. Cover the breast with six slices of
streaky bacon. Place the bird in a roasting-tin and cover with
foil if you do not have one of those admirable self-basting tins.
Cook for one and a half hours or more, according to the size of
the bird; put it in a hot oven for twenty minutes, then reduce
the heat to moderate. On no account let the bird become dry.
It should be plump and succulent when brought to the table.
Bread sauce (p. 19) and small sausages are the usual accompaniments.

Chicken in Aspic

This is an easily made dish and a useful standby for a summer
supper party.

1 *large or 2 small chickens*   1 *dessertspoon chopped celery*
1 *or 2 small onions*   *tops*
2 *dessertspoons chopped*   *water*
   parsley   *salt and pepper*

Cut the chicken into pieces and put them into a pan with the
finely chopped onion, one dessertspoon of chopped parsley,
and the celery tops. Season with salt and a grind or two of
black pepper. Barely cover with water and stew gently until
the chicken bones can be removed easily. Half an hour in a
pressure cooker should be enough. When cool enough to handle,
remove all the skin and bones from the chicken and lay the flesh
in a suitable mould. A ring mould is ideal. Sieve the liquor,
stir in the rest of the finely chopped parsley, pour it over the

chicken and leave to set in a cool place. When nearly cold, put into the refrigerator until needed. To serve, turn out of the mould and garnish with lettuce leaves and quartered tomatoes. If cooked with too much water, the addition of aspic may be necessary, but with the right amount, according to the size of the bird, it should jell perfectly.

Chicken Liver Paté (1)

This recipe is given for using up the livers of two chickens. If a larger quantity is required, chicken livers may be bought by the pound, in which case the amount of onion and butter should be adjusted.

2 *chicken livers*	*butter* or *clarified chicken fat*
1 *shallot*	*salt and pepper*

Trim and chop the liver rather roughly. Have ready a very finely chopped shallot and a knob of butter sizzling in a sauté pan. Ideally, the butter should be clarified chicken fat, but fresh butter will do as well. Fry half the onion in the butter to extract the flavour and remove before putting in the chopped liver. Sauté lightly and when it has just changed colour remove and pound to a paste with a pestle and mortar with the rest of the chopped onion. Add salt and pepper to taste and serve on buttered toast. This paté must be freshly made and will not keep.

Chicken Liver Paté (2)

8 *oz. chicken livers*	4 *rashers streaky bacon*
4 *oz. mushrooms*	1 *tablespoon brandy*
4 *oz. butter*	*salt, black pepper*

Chop the livers roughly and sauté them very lightly in two ounces of butter. Lift them out of the pan and put them on one side to keep warm. Sauté the mushrooms in the same butter for a few seconds with the chopped bacon. Season with salt and a good grind of black pepper and put the livers, mushrooms and bacon into an electric blender with the remaining two ounces of butter and the brandy. When quite smooth pot and seal down with melted butter. This paté will keep a week; it should be removed from the refrigerator at least one hour before serving.

Chicken and Mushrooms

2 *small chickens*	*stock from the giblets*
salt, pepper and a pinch of ginger	4 *oz. mushrooms*
3 *oz. butter*	*flour*

Cut the chickens into serving pieces and rub them over with mixed seasoning. Flour them heavily and brown quickly in the butter. Lift out the pieces of chicken and put them into a fire-proof dish with the mushrooms. Stew the giblets and pour the stock over the chicken. Cover closely and cook in a moderate oven for one hour. Remove the chicken to a serving-dish and keep it warm while you thicken the sauce if necessary and pour it over the chicken.

Chicken Pie

1 *large chicken*	5 *crushed peppercorns*
water	4 *oz. ham (uncooked)*
1 *carrot*	4 *oz. mushrooms*
1 *onion*	6 *oz. rough puff pastry (p.*
6 *cloves*	*167)*
faggot of herbs	1 *egg*
(parsley, thyme, 1 bay leaf)	1 *teacup cream*
salt	

Put the chicken and the giblets into a saucepan, cover with cold water and bring to the boil. Skim thoroughly and add the carrot cut in half, the onion stuck with cloves, the faggot of herbs, salt and finely crushed peppercorns. Simmer until the chicken is quite tender and let it cool in the liquor. When cool enough to handle, carve the chicken into strips and lay them in a pie dish with the diced ham and sliced mushrooms. Pour in the strained chicken broth until the dish is three-quarters full, put in a pie funnel, cover with rough puff pastry and gild the top with beaten egg. Bake in a hot oven for about half an hour, until the pastry is golden, and twenty minutes before serving pour in the cream through the pie funnel.

If there is any liquor left after stewing the chicken, return it to the pan with the chicken bones and boil it up for chicken stock.

Stewed Chicken

1 *chicken*	1 *tablespoon chopped mint*
1 *large onion*	2 *tablespoons chopped parsley*
water	*salt and pepper*

Limb the chicken and break the carcase in two pieces. Chop the onion roughly, the parsley and mint finely and put into a pan with the chicken. Add seasoning and barely cover with water. Bring to the boil and simmer gently about one hour according to the size and age of the chicken. Serve with plain boiled potatoes.

This recipe is very suitable for pressure cooking which retains the full flavour of the chicken.

Chicken with Tomatoes

1 *large chicken*	1 *teaspoon salt*
2 *onions*	$\frac{1}{4}$ *teaspoon cayenne*
4 *oz. butter*	1 *teaspoon sugar*
1 *wineglass Madeira*	$\frac{1}{2}$ *teaspoon cinnamon*
1 *teaspoon tomato paste*	6 *tomatoes*

Limb the chicken and cut into serving portions or ask your poulterer to do it for you. Rub each piece with salt and pepper and put aside. Chop or grate the onions finely and let them sizzle in butter for a few minutes. Brown the pieces of chicken in butter and put them into the pan with the onions. Dissolve the tomato paste in the wine and pour over the chicken in the pan, season with salt, cayenne, sugar and cinnamon, cover closely and cook slowly for three-quarters of an hour or until the chicken seems tender.

Halve and grill the tomatoes and arrange them round a serving-dish. Put the chicken in the centre, swill the pan out with a little Madeira and pour it over the chicken.

Spatchcock Chicken

Small birds, sometimes called *poussins*, are needed for this dish.

3 *small chickens*	*lemon juice*
salt and pepper	*butter*

Split the birds in half, flatten them on a board and skewer them in position. Rub them with salt and pepper, sprinkle with lemon juice and leave them for half an hour. Brush with melted butter and grill on both sides until cooked (about twenty minutes). If necessary, brush with butter from time to time to prevent the chicken from drying up. Serve with lemon quarters and a watercress or plain green salad.

Duck

Duck should be from ten weeks to three months old and weigh between five and six pounds, while a duckling should be only seven or eight weeks old and weigh under four pounds. Ducks need no hanging and may be killed and eaten the same day. Frozen birds have little flavour. There is deceptively little meat on a duck and it is as well to buy two if you have more than four or five people to serve.

Roast Duck

young duck	*butter*
oil	*sage and onion stuffing (p. 37)*
salt and pepper	*small glass red wine*

Choose a plump young bird not more than three months old. After that they start to get thin and tough. Allow fifteen minutes to the pound cooking time. A good-sized duck will take up to two hours.

Rub the bird over with oil, salt and pepper and butter the breast well. Put the giblets in a stewpot, cover with water and put them in the oven to extract all the juices for the gravy. Stuff the duck with sage and onion stuffing, using very little bread, if any. If preferred, the stuffing may be cooked separately in a flat dish when it will be brown and crisp. A self-basting tin is useful for the hostess-cook as the bird must be basted frequently or the breast will be dry, and a self-basting tin does the job without the duck having to be watched all the time. Put the bird in a hot oven to begin with, then reduce the heat to moderate until the bird is done. Remove any covering from the bird for the last half hour of cooking to crisp and brown the skin.

To make the gravy, remove the bird to a serving-plate and keep warm. Pour off any surplus fat and swill the roasting-tin with the giblet stock and a little vegetable water if the stock is not enough. Taste for seasoning, then boil rapidly over a fast heat stirring and scraping the juices run from the bird with a wooden spoon. A small glass of red wine will improve the flavour, or make an orange sauce (p. 25). When it is ready, pour into a gravy boat and keep hot until ready.

Apple sauce (if orange sauce is not served), garden peas, and boiled new potatoes or dry baked potatoes are the traditional accompaniments to roast duck.

Stewed Duck with Wine

1 *duck*	1 *wineglass Madeira*
2 *sprigs of fresh sage*	1 *small lemon*
1 *Spanish onion*	*salt and pepper*
1 *oz. butter*	½ *teacup water or stock*

Put a lump of butter with the sage inside the bird. Rub the duck over with butter, salt and pepper and put it in an earthenware pot. Chop the onion finely and put it round the bird. Add the roughly chopped giblets and stock, put on a lid and cook slowly in a moderate oven for one and a half hours. Pour in the wine and cook for a further half hour. Squeeze the juice of a lemon over the duck before serving, and serve with an orange salad (p. 162).

Wild Duck

Wipe the bird inside and out with a damp cloth rung out in vinegar. If the duck has been a fish eater it may be necessary to sear the inside of the bird to get rid of the fishy taste. Salt and pepper the inside and put in a lump of butter with a bunch of mixed herbs or a couple of sprigs of rosemary. Cover the breast with butter and several slices of streaky bacon and put to roast in a fast oven for fifty to sixty minutes. Baste from time to time with fresh orange juice. Garnish with orange slices first dusted with caster sugar and then fried in butter.

Serve with special sauce (p. 32) and orange salad (p. 162).

Roast Goose

goose	*salt and pepper*
stuffing (see below)	*flour*
1 *cooking apple*	

Allow fifteen minutes to the pound and fifteen minutes over. A ten-pound goose should take about two and a half to three hours to cook, and should serve eight people. A goose may be stuffed with herbs, sage and onion, mashed potato, or apple stuffing (see Chapter 3), or simply rubbed over with half a lemon with a peeled lemon placed inside. A sour apple cut up and put in the roasting-tin improves the flavour of the gravy.

Rub the stuffed goose with salt and pepper and dredge with flour, and put into a hot oven. After half an hour, lower the heat to moderate and cook until the bird is tender and well browned. Remove from the oven and keep the goose hot while the gravy is being made. Carefully pour off most of the fat and keep. Use the stock in which you have stewed the giblets for the gravy; pour it into the roasting-tin, scraping the dish well, and strain before serving.

Apple sauce (p. 17) is usually served with goose but other fruits may be used. Fried apple rings or fresh pineapple make a good garnish.

Grouse

Grouse should hang from three days to a week according to the weather and how high you like your game.

Even the youngest grouse is a dry little bird and needs to be well larded and basted during the cooking. The recipe given for roast grouse is the classic manner of cooking but they may also be stuffed with grapes, whortleberries or bananas.

Larding really means the insertion of strips of pork fat, called lardoons, into meat to make it more succulent, and for this a larding-needle is used but this is not often done these days and I have used the term above to indicate that the butter should be spread thickly over the bird.

Roast Grouse

Grouse are at their best plainly roasted unless badly shot or old, when they may be casseroled, potted or made into a pie. Allow one young grouse each.

Tie slices of fat bacon over the breasts which have been buttered and rubbed over with salt and pepper. Roast for thirty minutes in a moderately hot oven, basting frequently. Stew the giblets for gravy, made by swilling the giblet stock round the roasting-pan and seasoning if necessary. A splash of sherry is an improvement.

Mash the liver with a little of the stock and spread the liver on squares of bread, fried in butter, on which the grouse are served. Garnish with watercress and serve with gravy, bread sauce, breadcrumbs fried in butter and fried potato wafers.

Grouse Pie

For this dish, older birds may be used. It is quite unnecessary to use young ones which are at their best plainly roasted.

2 *grouse*	4 *oz. mushrooms*
flour	*salt and pepper*
1 *medium onion*	*water*
1 *lb. rump steak*	1 *wineglass port*
brandy	*rough puff pastry (p.* 167)

Split the grouse and wipe them with a damp cloth. Dust the birds with flour and place them in an earthenware oven dish with the sliced onion and the steak, cut into pieces. Add the mushrooms and season with salt, pepper and a dash of brandy. Barely cover with water. Put a lid on the dish and cook for one or two hours according to the age of the birds. Add the port and allow to cool a little before covering with pastry. Put the pie back into a hot oven and cook for about half an hour until the pastry is golden.

Grouse Casserole

1 *grouse per person*	12 *shallots*
butter	$\frac{1}{2}$ *lb. button mushrooms*
salt and pepper	*small glass red wine*
streaky bacon	

Allow one grouse for each person. Being small rather dry little birds they require slow cooking.

Wipe the birds with a damp cloth and put one shallot and a small knob of butter, salt and pepper inside each one. Butter the breasts well and wrap a strip of streaky bacon round each bird, tying it in place if necessary.

Place the birds in a wide casserole, preferably earthenware, and having peeled about a dozen shallots, wiped and trimmed half a pound of button mushrooms, put them into the casserole round the birds. Season with more salt and freshly ground pepper over the vegetables. Add a small glass of red wine, cover the casserole and cook in a moderate oven for about two hours or until the birds are tender.

Serve with potato sticks and a green salad.

Potted Grouse

If grouse are plentiful and cheap they may be potted and kept up to a month in a dry cold larder or a refrigerator. Pigeons, partridges and pheasant may all be treated in the same manner.

grouse	*salt and black pepper*
powdered cloves and mace	*butter*

Clean the birds carefully and wipe them dry. Season them well, inside and out, with powdered cloves, mace, freshly ground black pepper and salt and put them breast down into a stone pot. A hot-pot dish will do admirably. Put in plenty of butter, make the pot airtight and let them bake in a slow oven for at least two hours according to age. When the birds are cooked enough to remove the flesh easily from the bones, lift from the pot and let the butter go cold. Cut the meat in fillets as it comes off the bones, or mince and pound it fine, and put into well-buttered pots, press well down and add the butter from the pot but not the gravy. Cover with melted butter at least a quarter of an inch thick to keep.

The gravy underneath the butter in the pot may be used as a basis for game soup.

Jugged Hare

Ask the butcher to joint and bleed the hare into a basin.

1 *hare* or *leveret*	6 *peppercorns*
2 *oz. flour*	2 *onions*
2 *oz. butter*	8 *cloves*
a faggot of herbs	*salt*
(*thyme, parsley, sage*)	*water*
1 *bay leaf*	2 *wineglasses port*

Wipe the jointed hare over with a damp cloth. Flour the pieces and put them into a heavy-bottomed pan containing melted butter. Brown the hare, turning frequently. Add peppercorns, herbs and the onions left whole and stuck with cloves. Season with salt. Barely cover with water and bring to the boil slowly. Skim if necessary and simmer gently for two hours, when the hare should be nearly cooked. Stir in the blood and thicken the sauce. Add the port fifteen minutes before serving.

Red currant jelly (p. 237) or cranberry jelly (p. 230) is usually handed with jugged hare.

Partridge

Young birds are usually roasted but older birds tend to be tough and dry and are therefore better casseroled. As with the pheasant the end wing feather gives away the bird's age by being round if old and pointed when young. Also, the thicker the circle of red round the eyes the older the bird. Partridge should hang for four days and a week is not too long for those who like a gamey flavour.

1 *partridge per person*	*rashers of fat bacon*
butter	*slices of bread*
salt and black pepper	

Pluck, singe, clean and truss the birds, allowing one per person. Put a large knob of butter inside each bird, season with salt and black pepper and tie a rasher of fat bacon over the breast. Put them into a roasting-tin in very hot butter and cook in a hot oven about twenty minutes. Cut off the bacon about five minutes before the birds are done to let the breasts get brown.

Cut the crusts from as many slices of bread as you have partridge and fry them in butter. Place the birds on the bread, pour over the butter and juices from the pan; garnish with watercress and serve with bread sauce and fried crumbs.

Pheasant

Pheasants should be hung in a good larder, and in cold clear weather will keep for two to three weeks. If you have no larder then ask your poulterer to do you a favour and hang the bird for you and pluck it when it is ready, which is when the tail feathers 'give' on being pulled. A brace will serve up to six people.

Roast Pheasant

pheasant	3 *or* 4 *slices bacon*
butter	

Choose a plump young bird, spread thickly with butter and put a good knob inside the carcase. Three or four slices of bacon on the breast will serve to keep the bird moist. Roast in a basting tin with a lid in a hot oven for the first fifteen minutes until the bird begins to sizzle. Then reduce the heat to moderate for a further forty-five minutes, removing the lid for the last ten minutes so that the skin becomes brown and crisp.

Make a good gravy by swilling some vegetable stock round the roasting-tin, scraping the browned bits off the bottom. Season to taste and boil for a few minutes stirring with a wooden spoon. Serve with game chips and brussels sprouts or braised celery.

Casseroled Pheasant

The pheasant being a rather dry bird, the most succulent method of cooking to my mind is the following:

1 *pheasant*	4–6 *rashers bacon*
12 *shallots* or *pickling onions*	2 *oz. butter*
1 *lb. young carrots*	*salt and pepper*
4 *oz. mushrooms*	

To prepare the bird, dust the inside with salt and pepper and insert a shallot and a lump of butter the size of a walnut. Singe and truss as for roasting and lard the breast heavily with butter. Put the bird in an earthenware casserole and surround it with the peeled shallots and thinly sliced carrots and wiped mushrooms. Arrange the bacon rashers over the breast of the bird, put on a lid and place in a hot oven, then reduce the heat to moderate after half an hour. Cooking time should be about one and a half hours or more according to the age of the bird.

Serve with dry baked potatoes (p. 153) and a watercress salad.

Braised Pigeon

If you have to dress them yourself, dip the birds in boiling water and the feathers will come away easily.

3 *pigeons*	1 *dessertspoon flour*
3 *tangerines*	$\frac{1}{2}$ *pint Marsala*
6 *oz. butter*	*faggot of herbs*
6 *shallots*	*salt and pepper*
1 *small onion*	

Remove the pith and peel of as many tangerines as you have birds to cook and put one inside each bird with a lump of butter. Brown the birds in butter and place them in an earthenware oven dish with a lid. Sauté the shallots and finely sliced onion until transparent and add to the pigeons, mix the flour with a little of the Marsala and add to the contents of the dish. Lastly, put in the faggot of herbs, pour in the Marsala, see that the lid fits tightly and place in a moderate oven for one and a half hours or more, according to the age and size of the birds. Serve with small grilled sausages and little rolls of grilled bacon.

If tangerines are not available, use grapes instead.

Stewed Pigeon

3 *pigeons*	$\frac{1}{2}$ *pint stock*
$\frac{1}{2}$ *lb. rump steak*	*salt and pepper*
4 *oz. butter*	1 *tablespoon red currant jelly*
2 *rashers bacon*	1 *tablespoon lemon juice*
4 *oz. mushrooms*	1 *tablespoon flour*

Halve the pigeons and cut the steak into serving pieces. Brown the birds and steak in butter with the bacon cut into small pieces. Place in a casserole with the sliced mushrooms, stock and seasoning. Cover and allow to stew gently for one and a half hours. Add the red currant jelly, lemon juice and the flour blended with a little cold water and cook for another fifteen minutes.

Snipe

1 *snipe per person*	*streaky bacon*
salt and pepper	*hot buttered toast*

Snipe will keep for several days. They are very small birds and like woodcock, should not be drawn before cooking. They should be seasoned and very lightly roasted with a rasher of bacon round the breasts. Fifteen minutes in a hot oven should be enough and they are usually served on hot buttered toast, with a clear gravy, fried potatoes and salad.

Roast Turkey

Although turkey is usually reserved for the traditional Chrismas dinner, it is often more appreciated a month before the great day. Thanksgiving for the Americans falls on the last Thursday in November which is when they eat turkey.

turkey	*butter*
stuffing (*see below*)	*salt and pepper*

A turkey can weigh anything from six to thirty-six pounds, but the smaller the tastier. There should be very few pin feathers on a well-dressed bird.

For a bird weighing under fourteen pounds, allow fifteen minutes per pound and fifteen minutes over. About two and a half hours should be right for a ten-pound bird. Although it is usual to stuff a turkey, a young bird can be very good simply roasted and without any stuffing at all.

Fill the pouch of the bird with chestnut stuffing and the inside with sage and onion stuffing, sausage meat or forcemeat (see Chapter 3). Rub the breast of the bird with butter, salt and pepper and cover with foil. Place the bird in a fast oven for half an hour then reduce the heat to moderate. Baste frequently and put sausages to cook round the bird half an hour before it is ready.

Venison

Venison has been out of favour for many years except in Scotland but now, with the increasing interest in traditional English cooking, it can be obtained in London and other parts of the country. For my taste, it is too strongly flavoured meat but for those who do like it here are two recipes.

It is a lean and rather dry meat, and must be hung at least ten days before it is fit to eat. This gives it tenderness and flavour. The haunch, loin, leg and saddle are the most suitable cuts for roasting while the forequarter is better for stewing.

Roast Venison

The meat should be larded or marinaded before cooking. To lard the meat you will require a larding-needle threaded with strips of belly pork to stitch into the meat. Some butchers sell lardoons ready for use.

To marinade the meat, lay it in a deep dish with a cover and pour the following marinade over it and leave for twenty-four hours, turning it over from time to time.

½ *pint red wine*	12 *peppercorns*
½ *pint wine vinegar*	1 *sliced lemon*
½ *pint salad oil*	1 *small onion finely chopped*
salt and pepper	1 *tablespoon any chopped*
2 *bay leaves*	*herbs available*

Put the meat in a roasting-tin, pour the marinade over it and cover with foil. Cook for fifteen minutes in a hot oven to seal in the juices then turn the heat down to moderate. Allow half an hour to the pound and baste frequently while cooking.

POULTRY AND GAME

An alternative method is to bake the meat in a flour and water
dough. Cooked in this manner, it obviates the need to baste
but takes longer to cook. The crust should be removed half an
hour before the meat is ready to serve.

Red currant jelly (p. 237), cranberry sauce and wine gravy are
usually served when the meat is eaten hot and Cumberland
sauce if it is to be served cold (for sauces see Chapter 2). Pickled
aromatic plums (p. 223) are delicious served with venison.

Venison Stew

2–3 *lb. venison*	½ *pint stewed cranberries*
½ *lb. streaky bacon*	2 *cloves*
6 *small onions*	1 *bay leaf*
½ *bottle red wine*	½ *teaspoon chopped thyme*
black pepper and salt to taste	

Fry the bacon in a heavy pan until the fat has run, lift from the
pan and put aside. Cut the meat into chunks the size of a
walnut and brown them in the bacon fat for about eight
minutes. Add the chopped onions, spices and seasoning. When
the onions have softened add the cranberry preserve, the
wine and the bacon. Simmer very slowly for four hours, adding more wine if necessary. The meat should fall apart when
done.

Roast Woodcock

1 *woodcock per person*	*slices of bread*
salt and black pepper	*butter*
slices of streaky bacon	*brandy* or *burgundy*

Truss and clean but do not draw the woodcock, season them
with salt and freshly ground black pepper, and wrap them in
thin slices of streaky bacon. Have a slice of bread ready for
each bird and pour some melted butter over each slice. Let the

bread cool, then spread thickly with more butter. Put the birds on the slices of bread and place them in a hot oven.

Shortly before serving, take them from the oven and gather all the juices that have run from the birds and spread on the slices of bread. Put the birds back in the roasting-tin, pour over them a little brandy or burgundy, remove the bacon and return to the oven to finish cooking. Serve on the hot bread slices with a watercress and orange salad (p. 163).

9. Vegetables

British conservatism towards vegetables, regarding their only value an accompaniment to meat, misses the delectable pleasures of a wide variety of food. The gloomy sight and pervading odour of sodden cabbage, overboiled beans and cauliflower is only too well known. Not only are they un-attractive to the eye and palate but devoid of any food value, for any vitamins and minerals they ever had are boiled out and thrown down the sink.

A little care and imagination with even the humblest vegetable is repaid a hundredfold and can turn a mundane dish into a delight.

Vegetable 'stock' sounds more interesting than vegetable 'water', but whatever we call it, remember it provides a valuable base for soups which can be made with little more trouble than the opening and heating of a tin and are a good deal more enjoyable.

Artichokes

Globe artichokes are an expensive delicacy on the English market and usually imported. Originating in Africa and said to have been a favourite with Antony and Cleopatra, they grow almost everywhere in a temperate climate and I have seen them flourishing in a sunny sheltered part of a Sussex garden. Belonging to the thistle family, the globe artichoke has an attractive greyish-green spiky leaf and a pretty purple flower.

It is easily digested and one of the few vegetables diabetics are allowed to eat.

No one seems to know why the Jerusalem artichoke is so named. I have not discovered any connection with Jerusalem and it certainly bears no resemblance either in taste or looks to the globe artichoke to which it is not even related botanically. One theory is that the word Jerusalem is a corruption of *girasola*, the Italian for sunflower which belongs to the same family. It looks like a knobbly potato and has a sweet nutty flavour.

Boiled Globe Artichokes

Cut the stems close so that the artichokes will stand. Put them into a pan of boiling salted water, with the juice of a lemon to prevent discoloration, for half to three-quarters of an hour. When they are ready, the leaves should come away easily. Usually served cold with an oil and vinegar dressing, they may be eaten hot like asparagus with melted butter or hollandaise sauce, but only the succulent part at the base of the leaf and the heart is fit to eat. Remove the choke which is hairy and inedible if the artichokes are large. Young ones may be eaten before the choke develops.

Boiled Jerusalem Artichokes

Before boiling, the artichokes should be scrubbed and rinsed well and left to soak in salted water for half an hour. Put them into a pan of cold salted water, bring to the boil and cook for twenty minutes or until they are tender, depending on size. When cool enough to handle, peel them and serve hot with a rich white sauce (p. 32). They also make a delicious soup (p. 58).

Fried Jerusalem Artichokes

Prepare and boil the artichokes as in the preceding recipe. When they have been peeled cut them into thin slivers and fry them in hot oil. Drain well before serving.

Asparagus

The Vale of Evesham in Warwickshire and the sandy soil of Formby in Lancashire are known for the excellent flavour of their asparagus and gourmets argue the merits of each. A most delicious and delicate vegetable, asparagus are often served with a hollandaise sauce or a dressing of olive oil and vinegar, but in my view they are at their best served hot with melted butter.

To prepare for the table, scrape the stalks, cut them into even lengths and tie them together in a bundle. Stand the asparagus heads up in a deep pan of boiling salted water and cook until the stalks are tender. Remove them carefully from the pan and put them on a serving-dish. Serve at once with a sauceboat generously filled with melted butter.

Beans, Broad

If you grow broad beans in the garden they may be picked while the pods are still so tiny that the flower has only just withered, roughly two inches long. Wash them and throw into a pan of boiling salted water and dish them up with butter as soon as they are tender.

Later, when they are bigger, the beans should be removed from the pod and boiled quickly in boiling salted water. If left too long on the plant the greyish skin of the bean becomes tough and rather bitter. They can of course be slipped out of their skins when cooked and served with butter, but this is a last resort.

It is usual to serve broad beans with parsley sauce (p. 29) as an accompaniment to baked or boiled ham. If they are to be served with any other dish, a sprig of summer savory in the cooking water is a great improvement.

Beans, French

French beans are at their best picked young as are all vegetables and boiled whole. Top, tail and wash them. Put them into a pan of salted boiling water and cook them until tender. According to the freshness of the beans they will take between ten and fifteen minutes. Pour off the liquor into a stock pot if you have one on the go or use for making gravy. Reheat the beans with a little butter and serve hot.

Green vegetables, including beans, should not on any account have bicarbonate of soda added to the boiling water. There is a mistaken idea that it will keep them green; it might, but they will be mushy and have lost any delicate flavour they had.

Beans, Runner

This variety of beans grows larger and longer than French beans and they have a rougher surface. To prepare for the pot, they should be well washed and left to drain in a colander for a while. Top and tail them with a sharp knife and remove the stringy part from either side of the bean. They are now ready to slice thinly slantwise or put through a bean slicer. Cook and serve like French beans.

To test whether the beans are fresh if you are buying them, bend one in two and if it snaps easily then they are fresh. If they bend and appear flabby they are not worth buying, though they can be rejuvenated a bit by steeping them in ice cold water for half an hour.

Beetroot

Beetroot are at their best gathered young and fresh from the garden when the tops also may be boiled like spinach. Served with an oil and vinegar dressing they are deliciously tender.

To prepare the beetroot, cut off the stalks leaving about one inch above the root, wash them well in cold water and put them into a saucepan. Cover with boiling salted water, add a dash of vinegar and simmer with the lid on the pan until tender. Drain and when cool enough to handle remove the skins. This is easily done with the thumb and forefinger. Serve hot with melted butter, a white sauce, an oil and vinegar dressing, or slice them and let them go cold in malt vinegar if the beetroot is required as a pickle.

Broccoli

Very like a cauliflower in shape, broccoli should be cooked in the same fashion. If the broccoli is small, well shaped and the buds are tightly closed, cut off the leaves and as much of the stalk as possible. Scoop a hole in the stem and put it stalk down in a pan containing half a pint of boiling salted water. Leave the lid off the pan. To prevent any odour put a thick slice of bread tied in muslin at the bottom of the pan. If the broccoli is fresh it will be ready in ten minutes.

If the broccoli is a large one it may be better, to ensure even cooking, to break off the flowers from the main stem before boiling. Serve with melted butter or a little olive oil and a squeeze of lemon juice.

The flowers are also very good if they are fried in fresh butter after boiling them.

Brussels Sprouts

Appearing in the Belgian markets since 1213 brussels sprouts have long been known in England where, like the common cabbage, they do not always get the respect they deserve.

Choose tightly closed firm sprouts of even size, trim the stalk end with a sharp knife and remove any loose leaves. Throw them into a bowl of lukewarm salted water and leave them to stand for ten minutes. Put them into a pan and barely cover with boiling water, add salt to taste and cover them tightly. Boil quickly for seven or eight minutes. If they are overboiled they are ruined. A grate or two of nutmeg or a sprinkle of sharp, grated cheese enhances the flavour.

Cabbage

Indigenous to Europe, the cabbage was known and highly thought of by the Greeks and the Romans who believed it pulled them together after overindulging in wine.

Cabbage water has an all-pervading odour very difficult to dispel. It may, however, be minimized by putting a piece of stale bread tied in muslin in the pan in which the cabbage is to be boiled.

Like any vegetable, savoy cabbage is not fit to eat when it is overcooked as it so often is. It should be barely covered with very fast-boiling water and cooked for not more than ten minutes so that it still has the 'bone' in it. Drain well and chop it with butter or brown it lightly in butter or olive oil in a frying-pan.

As well as the savoy cabbage, spring greens are only too frequently overboiled. They lose their fresh green colour and become dark and flabby while the fatal addition of bicarbonate of soda produces an unnatural colour and causes the disintegration of the vegetable as well as the loss of minerals and vitamins.

Cabbage, Red

1 *medium-size cabbage*   1 *lb. cooking apples*

1 *lb. onions*
2 *oz. demerara sugar*
2 *cloves garlic*
1 *piece of dried orange peel*
a good pinch of allspice
powdered cinnamon, nutmeg
and any herbs the cook
fancies
1 *glass red wine*
2 *tablespoons wine vinegar*
salt and pepper

Cut the cabbage into quarters, remove the outer leaves if 'tired' and cut away the white core. Shred finely. Pare, core and slice the apples and the onions. Put them together in a large heavy pan or, if you wish, put into a casserole to cook in the oven. Add the sugar, crushed garlic and crushed orange peel. Season with the spices, herbs, salt and black pepper and pour in the red wine and vinegar. If it seems necessary, a little water may be added during the cooking time which should be about three hours over a low flame or in a slow oven.

Carrots

If the carrots are young and tender, cut off the tops, scrape them well and plunge them whole into boiling salted water. Add a teaspoon of sugar and cook until they are quite tender. Pour off the water, add a good knob of butter and toss them until they are well coated, glossy and shining. Put them into a heated serving-dish and strew them with finely chopped parsley.

When carrots become large and coarse they are still good for flavouring but the best way to serve them as a vegetable is to cut them into pieces, boil them and reduce them to a purée. Add some butter and a little fresh cream and serve very hot.

Carrots and Turnips

Scrape and slice the carrots and turnips, which must be young and tender, and put them into boiling salted water to cook for about ten minutes. Drain and chop them finely with a sharp knife until the vegetables are like little crystals, but do not on any account mash them. Add some butter, salt and pepper and serve hot. This is a North Country dish which I remember eating as a small child in my grandfather's house.

Cauliflower

One of the prettiest of vegetables, the cauliflower needs very little cooking. Eight minutes should be quite enough in a mere cupful of boiling salted water. It is delicious served with a cheese sauce poured over it and lightly browned under the grill, when it becomes a meal in itself. Or lightly fry the blanched flowerets in hot oil until golden brown.

Dressed with olive oil and lemon juice and eaten hot or cold, it is exceptionally good, but this is the Greek way of serving it, a tip the English cook may well take with advantage.

Celery

To make celery crisp, it should be put into a bowl of iced water with a few slices of lemon for one or two hours.

Celery, Boiled

Wash and trim the celery, cut the sticks into finger lengths and put them into a pan of boiling salted water. Simmer until the the celery is tender, then remove from the pan and drain well. Have ready a rich white sauce (p. 32) and pour over the celery before serving.

Celery, Braised

Wash the celery and cut the sticks into finger lengths. Put them into salted boiling water for ten minutes, drain and put them into a buttered baking-dish. Add some small pieces of butter and season to taste. Cover the dish and cook in a moderate oven for three-quarters of an hour or until tender. A little grated cheese brings out the flavour.

Leeks

March 1st is St. David's Day and on this date all good Welshmen wear leeks in their hats. When Cadwallen, King and Welsh leader, was about to meet Edwin, King of Northumbria, he ordered his men to wear leeks in their helmets to enable him to distinguish them from the enemy. The result of the battle was a victory for the Welsh and the choice of the leek as a national emblem. The French sometimes call them the asparagus of the poor.

Leeks, Boiled

Remove the root ends and green tops using only the white portion of the leeks. Split them lengthwise and wash in several changes of water. Tie them in small bunches. Cook in plenty of salted boiling water for about twenty minutes depending on the size and age of the leeks. Drain them well and serve with hollandaise (p. 24) or egg sauce (p. 23).

Leeks, Braised

Remove the root end and cut off the green part of the leeks which may be used for flavouring various soups. Wash them well, and cut into finger lengths. If they are too thick they may be split in half. Blanch the leeks in boiling salted water for five or ten minutes, drain them and put them into a well-buttered baking-dish. Add some shavings of butter, season with salt and pepper and a grate of nutmeg, cover and bake in a moderate oven for about one hour. Garnish with chopped parsley.

Marrow

The large variety grown to immense size in some English gardens and proudly displayed at the local horticultural show or harvest festival are not of much account on the table, but provided they are picked young and not too large the small variety widely grown on the continent provides a surprising number of delectable dishes. They grow prolifically in an English garden and the seed should be sown in the early spring so that a good crop is produced throughout the summer.

Picked young when the flower is still blooming, they are delicious boiled whole in salted water and served hot with a knob of butter, or they may be left to go cold and eaten as a salad with lemon juice and olive oil.

When they grow bigger, they make excellent soufflés. They are very good stuffed with minced meat spiced with herbs and onions and baked in the oven (p. 57). Sliced and fried in hot olive oil they make a good accompaniment to a meat dish.

Or, another good recipe: peel and cut the marrow into chunks about an inch and a half long, remove the seeds and put them into an earthenware casserole. Add some freshly ground pepper and some sea salt and a large knob of butter. Put a lid on the casserole and cook in a moderate oven for about half an hour. Dress with chopped parsley and serve hot. Other herbs such as sweet basil, thyme or cinnamon or nutmeg also may be used.

Mushrooms

The history of mushroom cultivation is almost as vague as the plant itself. Hippocratus and later Theophrastus made reference to the mushroom in 300 B.C., but the art of cultivating the plant in Europe was unknown until the time of Louis XIV, a great gourmet, when it was discovered that caves and abandoned quarries near Paris made ideal mushroom beds. From France the cultivation of the mushroom passed to England where it was first carried out in glass-houses. In recent years, cultivation has been extensive and mushrooms are now on the market all the year round. Field mushrooms, held by many to be unsurpassed for flavour, are a rarity nowadays and while there are several varieties of edible mushrooms, few people will eat any other than the cultivated mushroom and are afraid to try the chanterelle, puff-ball, parasol and other edible varieties.

Delicious eaten raw, cooked as an accompaniment to many dishes or used as a flavouring, mushrooms have a wide variety of uses. In preparing them for the pot it is better not to peel them though it is, perhaps, sometimes necessary. They may be washed and drained but it is better just to wipe them with a damp cloth before cooking.

Mushrooms with Cream

Wipe the mushrooms thoroughly. Do not peel or remove the stems unless absolutely necessary but slice them if they are large. Season with salt and freshly ground black pepper and put them with plenty of butter over a low fire. When the mushrooms are cooked add some fresh cream, heat and serve at once.

Mushrooms with Onions

Peel and decap one and a half pounds of good-size mushrooms. Put them into a baking-dish, sprinkle over them some finely chopped parsley, chopped spring onions, several dabs of butter, cover the dish and place in a moderate oven. Cook for thirty minutes and serve.

Stewed Mushrooms

When they are plentiful, mushrooms are delicious cooked in the following manner:

Slice the mushrooms thinly into an earthenware cooking-pot with a lid. Season with salt and freshly ground black pepper and add about one ounce of butter. Let them stew in their own juice for about half an hour, until cooked, and just before serving strew them with some finely chopped parsley. Serve them in the pot in which they have cooked as an accompaniment to meat stewed or roasted.

Onions

> . . . This is every cook's opinion
> No savoury dish without an onion
> But lest your kissing should be spoiled,
> Your onions must be thoroughly boiled.
>
> *Dean Swift*

Of all vegetables, the onion is the most widely used for flavouring. It has been a staple food for centuries and a shortage of onions in the kitchen sets the cook a real problem for there are few savoury dishes that do not call for the flavour of an onion.

Cooked or uncooked, onions have been used throughout the ages and recognized as a health-giving vegetable. Held in high esteem by the Romans, Pliny tells us that they used onions to cure the sting of serpents and other reptiles, and made poultices of onions and barley meal for the weak-eyed since it was believed that by drawing tears the onion cleared the sight. Onion juice was given to those who suddenly lost their speech.

'There were ruddy, brown girthed Spanish onions, shining in the fatness of their growth like Spanish friars . . .' Charles Dickens's mouth-watering description positively encourages us to go into the kitchen.

Plain boiled onions chopped with plenty of butter and black

148

pepper is a satisfying supper dish on a cold night. In Lancashire, onions are often served as a raw salad (p. 162) to accompany the Sunday joint of roast beef.

Baked Onions

Use Spanish onions if possible. They are sweeter and milder than any other variety. Remove the brown outer skin and wrap each onion in a square of foil. Put to cook in the hot ashes of a wood fire or in a moderate oven. Turn them from time to time and cook for about an hour until they are soft to the touch. Serve them smothered in butter.

Onions, Fried

Remove the outer skins of two large Spanish onions, slice them finely, dredge them with flour and fry them in smoking oil until crisp and golden. Drain them well, and serve at once.

Onions, Stuffed

Scoop out the centre of six large Spanish onions, put a knob of butter in each one and season generously with black pepper and a little salt. Fill the centres with equal parts of chopped chicken livers and cooked ham seasoned with a pinch of thyme and a grate of nutmeg. Place the onions in a well-buttered baking-dish and brush them with melted butter. Cover tightly and bake in a slow oven for about one hour or longer until soft. Just before serving add a glass of sherry to the liquor in the dish and serve at once.

Parsnips

Known in England even before the potato, parsnips are at their best after the first hard frost when the starch is converted into sugar and they become mellow and sweet. An excellent soup is made from parsnips and they are very good browned round a joint of roast beef.

Wash, scrape and cut the parsnips into finger lengths. Place them round the joint for about forty-five minutes and turn them from time to time until they are brown and crisp when they are ready to serve.

Parsnips, Boiled

Wash and scrape but do not peel the parsnips. If they are too big, cut them in half. Cook them in a saucepan without a lid, barely covered with boiling salted water, for thirty minutes or until they are tender, when they may be drained and mashed or sliced. Dress with melted butter and a little lemon juice and serve hot.

Peas

A common vegetable in the days of ancient Greece and Rome, peas were dried before use; it was left to the French to appreciate the delicate taste of shelled green peas and develop the *petit pois*, a very small sweet variety. The English developed a taste for a larger variety which when dried are known as marrowfat peas.

Of all frozen vegetables, peas are perhaps the most popular. Nevertheless, they cannot compare with freshly picked garden peas which are well worth the time and trouble entailed in shelling them.

Barely cover the shelled peas with boiling water, add one teaspoon of sugar, a good pinch of salt and a sprig of fresh mint. In ten minutes they should be ready. Drain off the water and put a piece of butter into the pan. Toss the peas until they are well coated with butter and remove the mint before serving.

Potatoes

The potato is so much a part of the British diet today that there are many to whom a meal is not a meal unless there are potatoes on the table.

It was the plunder of Peru which produced the first potato, the earliest mention of which we owe to Pedro de Ciaza de Leon who in 1538 discovered the plant in the Andes, where it was then cured by frost and dried instead of being cooked by heat. Its culture was highly developed, fertilized and irrigated and many varieties were grown. It was, and still is, the staple food of those Indians who live above the corn-growing zone.

It was probably between 1580 and 1585 that someone carried the potato to Europe, first to Spain, then to Italy; later it reached Charles l'Ecluse, keeper of the botanical gardens in Vienna. It took a long time to gain popularity despite the fact that Marie Antoinette wore its blossoms in her hair and Frederick the Great planted the potato in the Lustgarten. There was even a potato war in Germany.

It was the poor of Northern Europe, particularly in Ireland, who found that if there wasn't much else to eat, potatoes would keep body and soul together. Until 1844 Ireland had reasonably good crops, but it was the failure of the crop in that year and the subsequent potato famine in 1846 which caused nearly a million deaths from starvation and the emigration of more than a million and a half young people to New York during the next few years. As the blight spread to Germany and Poland, large numbers fled these countries for North America.

It is still a widely held fallacy that Sir Walter Raleigh or Sir Francis Drake brought the potato from Virginia to Ireland, but it did not grow in Virginia in their time. In fact, it was a group of Irish immigrants who took the potato back across the ocean and started its cultivation in the United States in 1719 having founded the town of Londonderry, New Hampshire, more than 130 years after Drake and Raleigh were supposed to have carried the potato from Virginia to Europe. The Raleigh legend is pure myth except to the romantic Irish and to the Germans who even have a statue to Drake in Offenburg with the inscription:

'Sir Francis Drake
Introducer of the Potato into Europe in
the year of our Lord
1580'

Still widely current, these canards were based partly on the ground-nut and partly on the sweet potato, a vegetable which has never appealed to the English as it has to the Americans.

Potatoes, Baked

If pricked with a fork before cooking, the potatoes will be mealy and the steam will escape more easily. An easier way still is to skewer them, since this makes them easy to handle. When washed and dried, rub them over with melted butter or olive oil and place them on a top rack in a hot oven for about one hour. Pinch them to see when they are ready and serve them in a folded white napkin.

Potatoes, Boiled

New potatoes are at their best scraped and put into boiling salted water which should be poured off as soon as they are cooked; they will take about ten minutes. Give them a shake in the open air if possible, if not, over a low flame. When the steam has been driven off, put in a sprig of fresh mint and a good knob of butter. Replace the pan lid for a few minutes and remove the mint before serving. Mint should never be boiled with potatoes: the potatoes become discoloured and the flavour of fresh mint is lost. Cooked in the manner described the full flavour of the potato and the mint is retained.

Old potatoes should be put in cold water, brought to the

boil and boiled gently for ten to fifteen minutes. They should be floury yet with 'the bone in them' and a sprinkling of chopped parsley improves the flavour and makes a nice garnish.

Potatoes, Chipped

Peel some large potatoes and cut them into chips not more than half an inch thick. Wash, drain and dry well before frying, a handful at a time, in very hot (390° F) oil or fat for eight to ten minutes. Drain them on greaseproof paper and serve them at once as they soon go flabby.

Potatoes, Dry Baked

Peel and halve some medium-sized potatoes and put them on a rack in a hot oven for thirty to forty minutes. Turn them once or twice while baking and when a light brown skin has formed a pinch with the fingers will tell if they are ready. If liked, the potatoes may be lightly floured before putting them in the oven, but this adds to the starch content and is not necessary. Send to table wrapped in a white napkin.

Potatoes, Mashed

In the old days, a wooden potato masher was used to get rid of the lumps and, if you happen to have one, it is still a very effective method. To ensure success, the potatoes should be dried thoroughly after boiling by shaking them well in the open air if possible, if not, over a very low flame. Put them through a ricer or an electric blender, though some potatoes tend to clog the machine. Return the potatoes to the pan, add salt and pepper and beat in a knob of butter and a little thin cream or milk with a wooden spoon until light and creamy.

Potatoes, Roast

Peel and halve medium-size potatoes and place them round the joint or in a separate baking-tin with hot oil, fat or dripping. Cook in a hot oven for about forty-five minutes, turning them occasionally, until they are brown and crisp. Serve at once.

Potatoes, Stuffed

6 *large potatoes*	*nutmeg*
2 *teacups chopped onion*	*salt and pepper*
¼ *pint thick white sauce (p.*	*milk*
32)*	2 *egg yolks*
butter	1½ *oz. grated cheese*

Scrub and oil six large potatoes and bake in the oven for about an hour until soft to the touch. Meanwhile cook two teacups of finely chopped onion in a little salted water, drain well and add a little thick white sauce. Keep it hot. Slice the top off the potatoes and scoop out the contents. Mash with butter, a dash of nutmeg, salt and pepper and a little milk. Beat until light and fluffy, add the slightly beaten yolks of two eggs, a little at a time. Refill the potato skins, leaving a hollow for the creamed onions. Sprinkle with grated cheese, and brown under the grill. Serve hot.

Salsify

Long and rather like a spindly white carrot, salsify is sometimes called oyster plant, vegetable oyster and 'John-go-to-bed-at-noon' because of its purplish-pink flowers which close at mid-day. The plant, a native of southern Europe, is more popular in America than it is in England. The young leaves may be used for salad or are delicious boiled.

Scrape the roots quickly and plunge them into a bowl of ice cold water with the juice of half a lemon to prevent discoloration. Cut into pieces, drain and place them in a saucepan. Cover with boiling salted water and one tablespoon of lemon juice. Bring to the boil, cover and cook for fifteen to twenty minutes or until tender. When cooked salsify taste rather like the oyster after which they have been named. They may be served plain with butter and chopped parsley or with a béchamel sauce, hollandaise (p. 24) or egg sauce (p. 23). They are also sometimes served mashed or scalloped. The liquid in which they have cooked makes a good soup base.

Shallot or Eschalot

This plant is said to have been introduced to England by the crusaders who found it growing wild in the vicinity of Ascalon in The Holy Land. Called 'the German onion' by some eighteenth-century writers, it is used in sauces, pickles, soups and made dishes, and as an accompaniment to chops and steaks.

Spinach

There have been many arguments in recent years as to whether spinach has much food value or whether it destroys the calcium in the human body. However, no conclusions appear to have been reached and it has been regarded as a body builder for more than twenty centuries.

Originating in Persia, it is mentioned in a fourteenth-century English cookery book and it was used in the kitchen of Richard II; Tusser wrote about it in 1557, and there is even a mention of it in Boswell's *Life of Johnson*.

It is a somewhat tiresome vegetable to clean, and this is most easily done after trimming by putting the leaves in a large bowl of cold water. Swill them round for two or three minutes, then lift them out when the mud and grit should have settled in the bowl. Repeat at least twice in cold water before lifting into the pan. Cook the spinach as the French do in plenty of boiling water or, as is often advised, in none at all, for about fifteen minutes; there are two opinions about boiling spinach and both are possible. Add salt to the water just before removing from the pan. This ensures that the spinach remains green. If cooked in salted water, the vegetable tends to discolour. It may be puréed and served with the addition of a grate of nutmeg and a little cream or left in the leaf and dressed with olive oil and lemon juice or tossed in melted butter.

Spinach Soufflé (1)

2 *tablespoons butter*	1 *breakfast cup milk*
2 *tablespoons flour*	2 *breakfast cups cooked and*
salt and pepper	*sieved spinach*
nutmeg	3 *eggs*

Melt the butter, stir in the flour and blend well without browning. Season with salt and pepper and a grate of nutmeg. Add the milk slowly, stirring all the time. Remove from the fire and stir in the spinach. This is where an electric blender is useful. Add three egg yolks, one at a time. Fold in three stiffly beaten egg whites, beaten with a pinch of salt, and turn into a buttered soufflé dish. Bake in a moderate oven for thirty or forty minutes when the soufflé should be well puffed and delicately browned on top. Serve immediately.

Spinach Soufflé (2)

Make a sauce as in the preceding recipe adding four tablespoons of grated cheese. Boil one pound of cleaned spinach for about fifteen minutes until tender, add salt, stir and drain. Chop the leaves roughly and place in a buttered soufflé dish. Beat three egg yolks into the cheese sauce. Fold in the stiffly beaten egg whites and pour over the spinach. Grate some more cheese over the top and cook in a moderate oven as above.

156

Swedes

Swedes should be peeled and cut into pieces and boiled for fifteen to twenty minutes in salted water until soft. Drain and mash them with plenty of butter and serve with stewed or roast meats. The swede really comes into its own in a Cornish pasty to which it is absolutely essential (p. 47).

Turnips

The turnip has been cultivated as a vegetable for hundreds of years. Early English herbalists mentioned it frequently and it has even been used in armorial bearings to represent a kindly disposed person who relieved the poor. Turnip tops contain a surprising amount of calcium, phosphorus and iron and are as valuable as milk in the diet. When young and tender, they are very good boiled in salted water, drained and served hot with a little butter or lemon juice.

Small white turnips should be scraped and put into boiling salted water to cook for fifteen to twenty minutes until tender. Drain them well, dust them with white pepper and shake them in a little melted butter. They are at their best young and fresh from the garden.

10. Salads

The golden rule of salad making is to use only the best and freshest of vegetables. Salads should not only look good but taste good also. Clean and crisp, practically any vegetable is good to eat raw but boiled and raw vegetables should never be mixed.

It is the usual habit of the British to serve salads only with cold meats, while on the continent they are served at nearly every main meal. In some parts of the continent salads are served first while you wait for the main course to be prepared, while in France it is usual for them to be served with the cheese course, after the main dish and before dessert. But at whichever stage of the meal a salad is served, it should 'freshen without enfeebling and fortify without irritating' to quote Brillat-Savarin.

Beetroot Salad

If you grow beetroot in the garden, pull them while the roots are small and the leaves are young and tender. Wash them well and cut off the leaves, leaving about an inch of stalk. Put them into a pan, cover with cold water and bring to the boil. Let them simmer until cooked through, which will take half an hour to an hour, then remove from the water and leave to drain. Put the leaves into the boiling water and when they too are tender, drain them well and serve together with the peeled beetroot. Dress with olive oil and vinegar or lemon juice.

To serve them raw, peel the beetroot with a sharp knife, shred them not too fine and dress with salt, pepper and lemon juice.

Cabbage Salad

Slice the hard heart of a cabbage very finely and place in a salad bowl. Mix three tablespoons of olive oil with two teaspoons of fresh lemon juice and salt and pepper to taste. Toss the cabbage in the dressing and serve at once. Garnish with shredded carrot or a few capers.

Red Cabbage Salad

Slice a small firm red cabbage heart finely and mix together with a thinly sliced Spanish onion. Toss the salad in a dressing of three tablespoons of olive oil, one dessertspoon wine vinegar, salt and pepper to taste. Never allow a salad to rest once it is dressed or it will go flabby.

Cauliflower Salad

Cauliflower is just as good to eat raw as it is cooked and some people prefer it that way.

Soak the sprigs of cauliflower in ice-cold salted water. Drain and dry thoroughly. Arrange them on a dish and serve with mayonnaise (p. 26) into which you have mixed a little tomato paste to give it colour.

Boiled cauliflower salad is equally good eaten hot or cold. Break the cauliflower into sprigs and prepare as above. Then plunge them into boiling salted water and cook them for a few minutes only. Take them out and leave to drain. Put them in a serving-dish and pour olive oil and lemon juice over them ten minutes before serving.

Celeriac Salad

Peel and wash the celeriac and shred it coarsely into a salad bowl. Stir in some well-seasoned salad cream (p. 30) and leave to marinate for at least half an hour before serving. Sprinkle with chopped chives just before serving.

Cucumber Salad

Choose a firm cucumber and slice it finely with or without the peel according to taste. Put into a dish, barely cover with malt vinegar and a dusting of salt and pepper. Garnish with chopped chives or fresh dill.

If the cucumber is bitter, remove the peel, slice it finely and put it into a colander. Sprinkle with salt, a tablespoon of vinegar, and leave it to drain out the bitterness. The cucumber will go a bit soft but it is more digestible if this is done. Pour a little cream or top of the milk on the cucumber and garnish with chopped chives.

Green Salad

By green salad is usually meant lettuce leaves or lettuce hearts cut in half and dressed with olive oil and wine vinegar, but watercress and cucumber are sometimes added.

Green Salad, Mixed

Pretty well anything fresh you can lay hands on can go into a green salad. Chicory, endive, celery, watercress, celeriac, fennel, sorrel, onion, escarole: the list is endless, but care must be taken to achieve what Evelyn calls 'Harmony in the composure of a sallet'.

Haricot Bean Salad

8 *oz. haricot beans*	*salt*
water	6 *spring onions*
1 *onion*	*fresh dill* or *fennel*
2 *tablespoons olive oil*	

Soak the beans in cold water for twenty-four hours. Next day drain them and put them into a saucepan with the finely sliced onion and olive oil. Season and cover the beans with water. Simmer for one hour or until the beans are soft and dry in the pan. Allow them to go cold before serving dressed with olive oil and lemon juice. Garnish with chopped spring onions and fresh dill or fennel leaves.

Lettuce Salad

As a general rule, never take a knife to a lettuce unless it is for the pot. If the leaves are too big for the salad bowl, tear them apart with your hands. If you cut them the edges will go brown when they come in contact with the vinegar in the dressing. Lettuce should be thoroughly cleaned, crisp and well dried before dressing. Keep the outer leaves of a Cos or London lettuce for the stock-pot or do as the Greeks do, shred them finely and toss them in plenty of olive oil and a little lemon juice. Never dress a green salad until the last possible moment, and preferably at table.

Serve the lettuce leaves in a china bowl. Some people like to rub the bowl with a garlic clove first, but do this only if you are sure your guests like garlic. The essence of the garlic gives a subtle flavour to the salad, but it must on no account be too pronounced. Just before serving, toss the leaves in a dressing of one part red wine vinegar to three parts olive oil mixed with a good pinch of salt and freshly ground pepper.

Onion Salad

As an accompaniment to roast beef this salad was always served at my father's table.

Choose a large Spanish onion. Remove the outer skin, slice the onion finely and marinate in four tablespoons of malt vinegar, one tablespoon of olive oil, salt, pepper and one good teaspoon of sugar. Prepare at least one hour before the meal and serve in the marinade. It is equally good with hot or cold roast beef.

Orange Salad

2 or 3 oranges	*1 tablespoon olive oil*
tarragon	*1 dessertspoon wine vinegar*
watercress	*1 teaspoon lemon juice*

Peel the oranges as you would an apple, using a very sharp knife and cutting as much of the pith away as is possible. Cut the fruit in thin slices crosswise, removing any pips. Arrange the slices in a salad bowl and sprinkle with chopped tarragon. Garnish with sprigs of watercress. Beat the olive oil, vinegar and lemon juice together and pour over the salad a few minutes before serving.

Potato Salad

New potatoes make the best salad but if the potatoes available are no longer very young, boil them in their skins. They will have more flavour and should not become floury. The secret of a successful potato salad is to pour the dressing over it while the potatoes are still hot so that it penetrates.

Boil or steam the potatoes and remove the skins as soon as they are cool enough to handle. Slice them carefully into a salad bowl and have ready a dressing of four tablespoons of olive oil, one tablespoon wine vinegar, salt and pepper. Beat very thoroughly before pouring on to the potatoes. Garnish with finely sliced spring onions or chopped chives.

Tomato Salad

Slice some firm tomatoes and dress with a good pinch of salt and three tablespoons of olive oil. Sprinkle with some dried winter savory or fresh chopped sweet basil. Vinegar or lemon juice should not be used with tomatoes which are quite acid enough in themselves.

Watercress and Orange Salad

Wash two bunches of watercress very thoroughly and let them dry. Remove the peel and pith from three or four oranges according to size and slice cross-wise into thin slices. Put them into a serving-bowl and dust with caster sugar. Just before the salad is sent to table, arrange the watercress in small bunches and dip in a well-mixed oil and vinegar dressing, then arrange around the oranges. Pour a tablespoon of the dressing over the oranges and serve.

11. Sweets, Puddings and Pies

If the English kitchen is famous for anything other than roast beef it is surely our puddings and pies. Since the days when Chaucer wrote in his *Canterbury Tales* of 'hote pyes' we have been making them with fish, meat, game and vegetables as well as fruit and preserves.

PASTRY

Good pastrymaking depends on a few simple rules. Never use self-raising flour or baking powder except for suet crust. Use very little water. Fold in as much air as possible, and handle as little as possible in a cool place, except for raised pie-crust pastry which must be made in a warm atmosphere. Always put pastry into a hot oven.

Flaky Pastry

The two important factors in making flaky pastry are the equal distribution of the butter and the rolling out of the pastry.

8 oz. flour	cold water
salt	lemon juice
6 oz. butter	

Sieve the flour and salt together and divide the butter into four equal portions. Rub one portion lightly into the flour until it is as fine as breadcrumbs. Mix in a little water and a squeeze of lemon juice until the pastry holds together. Turn on to a floured board and knead out any creases. Roll out to a strip six inches wide and cut another quarter of the butter into small pieces evenly over two-thirds of the pastry taking care not to put it too near the edges. Fold the pastry into three by placing the butter-free end two-thirds up the strip of pastry and bringing the other end over so that the butter-free end lies between.

Press the open ends lightly with a rolling-pin, dredge with flour and roll once more into a long strip. Repeat the process with the last two portions of butter and roll to the desired thickness.

Flan Pastry

When making a pastry shell, turn the flan tin upside down, oil it well and mould the pastry over the inverted tin. Prick the pastry lightly with the prongs of a fork and bake in a hot oven for fifteen to twenty minutes until cooked. Baked in this way, you will have a crisp flan case and there is no trouble about puffing in the middle or lining the case with beans which often leave the pastry a little sodden.

Quantities for an eight-inch flan:

4 *oz. flour*	1 *egg yolk*
a good pinch of salt	1 *teaspoon sugar*
3 *oz. butter*	*water to mix*

Sift the flour and salt together, add the sugar and rub in the butter with light fingers. Beat the egg yolk with a little water and mix into the flour. Knead lightly until smooth, roll into a ball and leave in a cool place for at least ten minutes before using.

Puff Pastry

8 oz. unsalted butter   lemon juice
8 oz. flour   cold water
salt

Leave the butter at room temperature for one or two hours before using. Sieve the flour with a good pinch of salt into a mixing-bowl. Take a piece of the butter about the size of a walnut and rub into the flour. Add a squeeze of lemon juice to lighten the pastry and enough water to make a dough. Form the dough into one piece, turn on to a floured board and knead thoroughly until it is smooth and velvety, and no longer sticks to the fingers. Roll the dough out rather thinly, shape the butter into a flat cake and place it in the centre of the dough. Fold the pastry loosely round the butter and roll out into a long strip. Now fold the pastry into three, folding the first flap away from you and the second flap towards you. Half turn the pastry until the folds are to one side. Press the edges with a rolling-pin to enclose all the air possible. This completes one turn; puff pastry requires seven turns and it should be placed in a cold place for fifteen minutes between each rolling and folding.

The secret of puff pastry is to keep the pastry cool and place it in a very hot oven to begin with to let the pastry puff. When it is well risen the heat of the oven should be lowered to finish the cooking.

Raised Pie Crust

1 lb. flour   1½ gills water or milk and
1 teaspoon salt   water
4 oz. lard   yolk of egg to glaze

Sieve the flour and salt into a warmed basin. Melt the lard in a small saucepan, add the liquid and bring to boiling point. Make a well in the flour, pour in the liquid a little at a time, and mix quickly to a paste. Turn on to a floured board and knead with the hands until smooth and free from cracks. Use at once in a warm place as the pastry hardens as it cools. Glaze with the beaten egg yolk.

Rough Puff Pastry

8 oz. flour   lemon juice
½ teaspoon salt   water
6 oz. butter

Sieve the flour and salt together into a mixing-bowl and add the butter cut into small pieces. Add the lemon juice and enough ice-cold water to make a stiff dough and turn on to a floured board. Roll out lightly into a long strip, fold into three, turn the pastry half round, seal the edges and roll again into a long strip. Repeat until the pastry has had four turns and cool thoroughly before use. If wrapped in foil or greaseproof paper, the pastry may be kept overnight.

Shortcrust Pastry

8 oz. flour   ¼ teaspoon salt
4 oz. lard or butter   water
or 2 oz. lard and 2 oz. butter

Sieve the flour and salt together in a mixing-bowl and cut in the lard. Using only the tips of the fingers, rub the lard into the flour until it resembles breadcrumbs. To get as much cold air as possible into the pastry, lift up the flour and lard in the hands before mixing with cold water into a firm dough. Knead lightly until free from cracks and roll out as required.

Suet Crust

4 oz. beef suet	2 teaspoons baking powder
8 oz. flour	water
½ teaspoon salt	

Free the suet from skin and shred it as finely as possible. Sieve the flour, salt and baking powder into a bowl, mix in the shredded suet and work to a soft dough with a little cold water. Turn on to a floured board, knead lightly and roll out as required. Suet crust should be used at once. It will not keep.

Apple Amber

This is an old-fashioned sweet dating back to 1700 and is very good today.

2 lb. cooking apples	4 oz. brown sugar
2 eggs	2 oz. butter
1 lemon	3 oz. caster sugar
4 tablespoons water	shortcrust pastry (p. 167)

Peel, core and slice the apples. Separate the yolks from the whites of the eggs. Grate the lemon rind and strain the juice. Stew the apples with the water until soft, then stir in the brown sugar, butter, lemon juice and grated rind and beat well. Beat the egg yolks lightly and stir into the apple mixture. Line a pie dish with pastry, prick the bottom with a fork and leave for ten minutes before pouring in the apple mixture. Place in the centre of a fairly hot oven and bake for half an hour when the pastry should be done.

Whisk the white of egg with half the caster sugar and a pinch of salt until it stands in stiff peaks. Fold in the remaining sugar

168

and pile it on the apples. Put it back in the oven for a further ten minutes to crisp the meringue and serve with thick cream.

Apples in Brandy

6 *apples*   1 *wineglass brandy*
honey

Choose a type of apple which will remain whole when cooked, for example Granny Smith or other eating apple. Pare the apples very carefully and remove the core. Arrange them in a wide pan and put one teaspoon of honey into each apple. Pour in a wineglass of brandy and put to simmer over a very low heat for about one hour. Cover the pan with a lid while cooking and baste the apples from time to time. When they are cooked remove from the fire and leave to cool. Lift them gently from the pan and arrange them on a serving-dish. Decorate with whipped cream. Serve very cold.

Apple Charlotte

$1\frac{1}{2}$ *lb. apples*   1 *lemon*
3 *oz. breadcrumbs*   4 *oz. sugar*
2 *oz. suet*   2 *oz. butter*

Peel and slice the apples. Mix together the breadcrumbs, shredded suet, lemon juice, grated lemon peel and sugar. Put a layer of apples in a buttered pie dish followed by a layer of the breadcrumb mixture and some shavings of butter. Repeat until the dish is full, finishing with a layer of breadcrumbs. Cut the rest of the butter into small pieces and place on top. Bake in a moderate oven for about one hour until the apples are cooked and the top is crisp and golden. Serve with custard (p. 22) or cream.

Apple Crisp

2 *lb. cooking apples*	4 *oz. butter*
6 *oz. sugar*	*salt*
8 *oz. flour*	½ *teaspoon cinnamon*
juice of 1 *lemon*	

Peel, core and slice the apples and stew them for fifteen minutes with two ounces of sugar, lemon juice and cinnamon. When they are cooked, put them into a buttered baking-dish. Cut the butter into the sifted flour and work it in until it is the texture of breadcrumbs. Add the sugar and a pinch of salt. Fork the mixture lightly over the apples and bake in a moderately hot oven for about half an hour until the top is crisp and golden. Serve with fresh cream.

This is also known as apple crumble. Any soft fruit may be used in place of apples.

Apple Dumplings (1)

There are two methods of making apple dumplings, by baking or boiling them. If they are to be baked, shortcrust pastry is used, but if they are preferred boiled, then suet crust is used. Allow one apple, not too large, for each person.

1 *lb. shortcrust pastry (p. 167)*	1 *tablespoon currants or raisins*
6 *cooking apples*	1 *small glass brandy or wine*
6 *good teaspoons soft brown sugar*	*water*
	caster sugar

Peel and core the apples. Fill the centres with sugar, currants and or raisins previously soaked in either brandy or wine to plump and soften them. Roll out the pastry thinly and cut into rounds large enough to wrap round each apple. Place each apple in the centre of the pastry, dampen the edges and gather round the apple. Place the dumplings, join downwards, in a baking-dish, brush with cold water and dust with caster sugar. Bake in a fairly hot oven for about fifteen minutes or until the pastry is golden, then lower the heat and bake for about half an hour more when the apples should be cooked.

Apple Dumplings (2)

1 *lb. suet crust (p.* 168)	6 *cloves*
6 *apples*	6 *teaspoons soft brown sugar*

Prepare the apples as in the previous recipe and stuff the centres with the sugar. Place a clove on top of each apple. Roll out the pastry in rounds that will cover each apple and see that they are firmly enclosed in the pastry. Wrap each apple in foil and drop them into a large pan of boiling, slightly salted water. Bring back to the boil and simmer gently for about fifty minutes. Lift from the pan and serve hot with single cream or custard (p. 22).

Apple Fritters

4 *oz. flour*	*salt*
$\frac{1}{4}$ *oz. butter*	4–6 *apples*
1 *egg*	*lard* or *oil for frying*
milk	

To make the batter, separate the egg yolk from the white and beat them separately. Beat the butter to a cream and add the egg yolk. Mix in the flour and salt and thin down with milk to a dropping consistency. Stand for at least an hour and just before using fold in the beaten white of egg.

Peel and core the apples, cut them into fairly thick slices and dip them in the batter. Drop them quickly into a deep pan of hot lard or oil and fry the apple slices until they are golden one or two at a time. Drain on greaseproof paper and pile them on a hot dish, strew with caster sugar and serve at once. If the apple slices are soaked in a syrup of wine, sugar and lemon juice first, the fritters will be ambrosial.

Apple Pie

shortcrust pastry (p. 167)	*butter*
1½ *lb. cooking apples*	*lemon juice*
3 *oz. sugar*	1 *teaspoon cinnamon*

Line a buttered oven plate with thinly rolled shortcrust pastry. Fill the plate with sliced cooking apples. Sprinkle with sugar, dot with butter, add a squeeze of lemon juice and a teaspoon of powdered cinnamon and cover with pastry. Trim and pinch the edges; make three small gashes in the top with a pointed knife and bake in a hot oven about one hour. Dredge with fine sugar and serve hot or cold.

In Lancashire and Yorkshire it is the usual practice to serve cheese with apple pie.

Apple Pudding

2 *lb. cooking apples*	6 *oz. white breadcrumbs*
4 *oz. butter*	½ *pint thick cream*
3 *oz. moist brown sugar*	1 *oz. plain chocolate*
1 *lemon*	

Peel, core and slice the apples finely. Put them in a pan with one ounce of butter, two ounces of sugar and the juice and grated rind of the lemon. Cook slowly and beat until soft and smooth. Fry the breadcrumbs in the rest of the butter and add the remaining sugar. Butter a shallow fireproof dish and put in a layer of apples, next a layer of breadcrumbs fried in butter, then another layer of apples and top with fried breadcrumbs. Cook in a hot oven until golden, ten to fifteen minutes. Let it go quite cold then whisk the cream until fairly stiff and spread over the pudding. Grate the chocolate over the top and serve chilled.

Apple Pudding (Boiled)

$\frac{3}{4}$ *lb. suet crust (p.* 168)	*juice of $\frac{1}{2}$ lemon*
2 *lb. cooking apples*	$\frac{1}{2}$ *oz. butter*
4 *oz. sugar*	$\frac{1}{2}$ *teacup of water*
salt	6 *cloves*

Roll the suet crust out thinly and line a buttered pudding basin, leaving enough for the lid. Slice the apples and fill the basin adding the sugar, cloves, lemon juice, butter, water and a pinch of salt. Damp the edges of the crust, put on the lid and pinch the edges firmly together to retain the juice. Cover with oiled paper or foil, tie down with a pudding cloth and boil for two or three hours. Provided the water is kept topped up, longer boiling will do no harm. Do not turn the pudding out but wrap a white napkin round the basin and serve with hot custard (p. 22). A dessertspoon of gin poured over each serving is delicious.

Plums, damsons, gooseberries, rhubarb and other soft fruit may be used in place of apples.

Apple Pudding (Baked)

2 *lb cooking apples*	4 *oz. moist brown sugar*
3 *oz. butter*	3 *eggs*
1 *teaspoon lemon juice*	*salt*
$\frac{1}{2}$ *teaspoon cinnamon*	2 *oz. breadcrumbs*

Stew the apples with the butter, lemon juice, cinnamon and sugar until the apples are soft and fallen. Remove from the fire and let them cool a little, then stir in the well-beaten eggs and a pinch of salt. Butter a baking-dish and spread a thin layer of breadcrumbs. Put in the apples and another layer of bread-crumbs. Add a few shavings of butter and bake in a moderate oven until golden brown, about twenty minutes. Sprinkle with caster sugar and serve hot with cream or custard sauce (p. 22).

Apple Sponge Pudding

1 *egg*	*pinch of salt*
weight of the egg in butter,	*2 lb. cooking apples*
caster sugar and self-rais-	*1 oz. sugar*
ing flour	*½ lemon*

To make the sponge, take the weight of one egg in butter, caster sugar and well-sifted self-raising flour. Cream the butter and sugar together, beat in the egg and slowly sift in the flour and a pinch of salt. Peel and slice two pounds of cooking apples and stew them with one ounce of sugar and the juice of half a lemon. When they are soft, turn into a buttered baking-dish and lay the sponge mixture over the apples. Bake for three-quarters of an hour in a moderate oven, when the sponge should be well risen and golden. Serve with a custard sauce (p. 22).

Baked Apples

6 *cooking apples*	*2 oz. Barbados sugar* or
1 *oz. sultanas*	*honey*
	water

Choose apples of good shape and equal size. Rinse them in cold water, core them carefully and score the peel lightly round the middle. Arrange them in a shallow baking-dish and stuff the centres with sultanas and sugar or honey. Add two tablespoons of water to start them cooking and bake in a moderate oven for three-quarters of an hour. Serve with fresh cream or rice pudding.

174

Another way is to prepare the apples as above but stuff the centres with two ounces of butter creamed with two ounces of Barbados sugar and half a teaspoon of powdered cinnamon, and instead of water to start the apples cooking use red or white wine.

Apricots with Rum

The best apricots for this delicious dish are the round dark dried kind, more expensive than the yellowish type but well worth the difference in price. One pound will serve six people.

1 *lb. dried apricots*	*pinch of salt*
lemon rind	1½ *tablespoons rum*
2 *tablespoons dark brown sugar*	

Soak for two or three hours in cold water (if they are soaked overnight, they will require less cooking time).

Using the same water they have been soaked in, add two or three slivers of lemon rind, two heaped tablespoons of dark brown sugar, a pinch of salt and put into an earthenware casserole with a lid. Stew in a very slow oven for about two hours. Ten minutes before serving, add one and a half tablespoons of rum and return to the oven for ten minutes uncovered to allow the spirit to evaporate. Serve with a bowl of thick or whipped cream. This dish is equally good hot or cold.

Bakewell Tart (or, traditionally, pudding)

6 *oz. shortcrust pastry (p.* 167) *or puff pastry (p.* 166)	2 *eggs*
raspberry jam	3 *oz. ground almonds*
2 *oz. butter*	*rind and juice of half a lemon*
3 *oz. sugar*	*milk*

Line a buttered pie plate with the pastry and spread with raspberry jam. Warm the butter and sugar together and beat in the eggs. Add the ground almonds, and the grated rind and juice of half a lemon. The mixture should be of a running consistency and if it is too thick, add a little milk. Pour the filling over the jam and decorate with twisted strips of pastry in a lattice pattern. Bake in a moderate oven for one hour.

Baked Custard

 1½ *pints milk*   *salt*
 3 *eggs*   *nutmeg*
 1½ *oz. sugar*

Heat the milk but do not let it boil. Beat the eggs and sugar together then stir in the warmed milk and a pinch of salt. Pour into an earthenware dish, grate a little nutmeg on the top and place the dish in a tin of warm water. Bake in a moderate oven for about forty minutes when the custard should have set. If the oven is too hot, the eggs will curdle and separate. Remove the dish from the tin of water and leave to cool.

Banana Custard

 6 *bananas*   1 *pint custard sauce* (*p.* 22)
 raspberry jam   *nutmeg*

Slice six bananas into a serving-dish and spread some raspberry jam over them. Prepare one pint of egg custard and pour it over the bananas. Grate a little nutmeg over the top and put in a cool place for the custard to set.

 This sweet, simply and quickly made, is a firm favourite with small children.

Batter Pudding

3 *eggs*	1 *pint milk*
3 *tablespoons flour*	1 *tablespoon lard*

Beat the eggs with the flour until very light. Then add the milk and beat again until bubbles appear. Some cooks leave their batter to rest awhile before cooking but this is not necessary. Heat a good tablespoonful of lard in a small roasting-tin and when a faint smoke rises from it pour in the batter and cook in a hot oven for about thirty minutes until it is well puffed, brown and crisp. Serve with lemon juice and sugar or warmed honey and powdered cinnamon.

Brandy Cream

Simple but expensive to make, this is a real party piece.

4 *tablespoons icing sugar*	4 *tablespoons brandy*
juice of 1 *large lemon*	2 *pints fresh thick cream*

Strain the lemon juice over the sugar and stir until the sugar is dissolved. Add the brandy and stir in the cream. Whisk until stiff but not too stiff and serve cold in a glass dish or individual jelly glasses.

Bread and Butter Pudding

6 *slices thin bread and butter*	1 *pint milk*
2 *oz. currants*	*salt*
2 *oz. sultanas*	*lemon peel or vanilla*
2 *oz. sugar*	*nutmeg*
2 *eggs*	

Arrange the thinly cut slices of bread and butter in a well-buttered pie dish with a layer of sugar, currants and sultanas

M   177

between each layer of bread and butter. Flavour the milk, either by infusing with a paring of lemon peel, or a stick of vanilla, and a pinch of salt. Whisk the eggs well and stir in the milk. Pour over the pudding and let it stand for at least one hour. Grate some nutmeg on top of the pudding and cook in a moderate oven about one hour. The top should be brown and crisp and the pudding moist and succulent. It is greatly enriched by serving with cream.

Canary Pudding

4 oz. butter	¼ teaspoon baking powder
4 oz. sugar	salt
2 eggs	milk
4 oz. flour	

Cream the butter and sugar together as if making a cake until light and fluffy. Beat in the eggs, one at a time and fold in the sieved flour, baking powder and a pinch of salt. If necessary add a little milk to give a dropping consistency. Put the mixture in a buttered pudding basin, cover with foil or greaseproof paper and tie down with a pudding cloth. Put the basin into a pan of boiling water and steam for one and a half hours or the equivalent in a pressure cooker. Serve with apricot (p. 17) or wine sauce (p. 32).

Caramel Cream

3 or 4 eggs	pinch of salt
6 tablespoons sugar	1 pint milk

Make a custard by beating three or four eggs according to size with three tablespoons of sugar, a pinch of salt and one pint of milk. Pour into a double boiler or a basin placed over a pan of simmering water and stir with a wooden spoon until thick. The custard should coat the spoon when ready. Dissolve three tablespoons of sugar in a shallow pan and when it is bubbling and dark but not burnt stir it quickly into the custard. Pour the custard into a mould and leave to go cold. Serve with fresh cream.

Caramel Custard

3 *eggs*	Caramel:
3 *tablespoons sugar*	2 *tablespoons sugar*
pinch of salt	1 *tablespoon water*
1 *pint milk*	*lemon juice*

Dissolve two tablespoons of sugar with one tablespoon of water in a thick saucepan with a squeeze of lemon juice. Boil the syrup carefully until it turns golden brown and frothy. It is very important that the sugar doesn't burn or the flavour of the pudding will be ruined. Pour quickly into a well-buttered ovenproof dish or cake tin; tip it round to coat well with caramel.

Beat the eggs with three tablespoons of sugar, a pinch of salt and the milk and pour into the caramel. Stand the pudding in a tin of hot water and bake in a very slow oven for about one hour until the custard has just set. When quite cold turn out of the tin on to a serving dish. The caramel will have melted and should run down the sides of the pudding. A dash of ratafia in the custard is an improvement.

Castle Pudding

4 *oz. butter*	4 *oz. flour*
4 *oz. sugar*	$\frac{1}{2}$ *lemon*
3 *eggs*	*strawberry jam*

Cream the butter and sugar together, beat the eggs until light and creamy and add a little at a time alternately with the sieved flour. Flavour with the juice and grated zest of the lemon.

Mix well and have ready some small moulds, well buttered, and three-parts fill them with the mixture. Bake in a hot oven for twenty-five minutes when the puddings should be well risen. Turn out of the moulds on to a serving-dish and top them with a good spoonful of jam. Serve hot with a hot jam or wine sauce (p. 32) and a sauceboat of cream or custard (p. 22).

Chocolate Mousse

6 *oz. bitter chocolate*	1 *teaspoon olive oil*
3 *tablespoons water*	3 *eggs*
1 *tablespoon strong coffee*	½ *pint thick cream*
salt	1 *oz. chopped almonds*

Break the chocolate into a saucepan and add three tablespoons of cold water. Place over a low flame and stir until the chocolate is thoroughly melted. Remove from the fire and stir in one tablespoon of strong coffee, a pinch of salt to bring out the flavour and one teaspoon of olive oil, then vigorously beat in the egg yolks, one at a time. Whip the cream until thick but not stiff. Stir in half the cream, the chopped almonds and fold in the stiffly beaten egg whites. Pour into a glass serving-dish, decorate with the remainder of the cream and serve very cold.

Chocolate Pudding

4 *eggs*	*milk*
1 *tablespoon flour*	3 *tablespoons caster sugar*
2 *oz. cooking chocolate*	

Beat the egg yolks and stir into them one good tablespoon of flour. Melt the chocolate with a little milk and add three table-spoons of caster sugar and three tablespoons of milk. Fold in the stiffly beaten egg whites, pour into a baking-dish and bake in a slow oven for half an hour. Serve hot with whipped cream or brandy sauce (p. 18).

Christmas Pudding

12 oz. sultanas	1 tablespoon black treacle
12 oz. currants	½ teaspoon salt
4 oz. candied peel	1 teaspoon mixed spice
8 oz. suet	½ teaspoon ground cinnamon
4 oz. flour	½ teaspoon ground ginger
4 oz. breadcrumbs	¼ nutmeg, grated
4 oz. ground or chopped	1 lemon
almonds	4 eggs
4 oz. brown sugar	brandy

To clean the currants, rub them between the hands with a little flour, chop the candied peel as finely as possible and soak the currants and sultanas in brandy. Shred the suet finely into a large mixing-bowl and add the flour, breadcrumbs, almonds and sugar. Next add the treacle, salt, spices, the juice and grated rind of the lemon and stir well before adding the well-whisked eggs, sultanas, currants, peel and more brandy if necessary to bring the mixture to a dropping consistency. Press well down into a buttered pudding basin, cover with greaseproof paper or foil and tie down with a clean pudding cloth. Boil for eight hours or until the pudding is very dark in colour. On Christmas Day, or when the pudding is to be eaten, boil for at least one hour before serving. Serve with rum sauce (p. 29) or brandy butter (p. 18). The amounts given should make a pudding for eight or twelve servings, but if a smaller pudding is required, use half the amounts given.

This pudding will come to no harm if kept for twelve months in a cool dry place and well covered, but it should be looked at from time to time and a little brandy added to keep it moist.

Cream Blancmange

½ oz. gelatine
½ pint milk
½ pint single cream

3 oz. sugar
pinch of salt
1 vanilla pod

Soak the gelatine in half the milk for ten minutes. Heat the rest of the milk with the cream, sugar and vanilla pod, stirring until the sugar is dissolved. At boiling point add to the gelatine stirring occasionally until nearly cold. Remove the vanilla pod and pour into a buttered mould to set. Serve with a bowl of cream.

Almond essence, coffee essence or chocolate may be used in place of the vanilla.

Cup Custard

1 pint milk
3 oz. sugar
1 vanilla pod
5 eggs

1 tablespoon brandy
salt
nutmeg

Warm the milk and sugar together in a saucepan. Put in the vanilla pod and steep for half an hour then remove the vanilla pod. Add a pinch of salt, heat the milk to boiling point, and strain into a clean basin. Whisk the eggs well and stir into the cooled milk. Strain into a bowl and place in a saucepan of boiling water over a low heat, or use a double saucepan. Keep stirring the custard one way only until it thickens and on no account allow it to reach boiling point or it will at once curdle. Remove from the fire and stir in the brandy. Pour into custard glasses, grate a little nutmeg over the top and serve cold. If preferred, the peel from half a lemon, or a bay leaf, may be used instead of the vanilla pod.

Custard Ice

Individual earthenware pots or ramekin dishes should be used for this sweet. Children love it.

6 *egg yolks*
3 *tablespoons sugar*
pinch of salt

1½ *pints milk*
1 *vanilla pod* or *bay leaf*
caster sugar

Beat the egg yolks with three tablespoons of sugar and a pinch of salt. Scald the milk with a vanilla pod or bay leaf and leave it to infuse for ten minutes. Remove the vanilla pod and stir the milk into the eggs. Strain into the pots and remove any froth. Stand the pots in a tin of warm water, cover and cook in a moderate oven for about thirty minutes until set. When the custard is firm, take out of the water at once and leave to become quite cold. Sprinkle the top of each pot thickly with caster sugar and place under the grill until the sugar has melted but not caramelized. Leave to cool before serving when the sugar will have set like ice. On no account put the pots into a refrigerator or the sugar will melt again.

Custard Pie

6 *oz. shortcrust pastry (p.*
   167)
4 *eggs*
1½ *pints milk*

4 *oz. sugar*
½ *teaspoon salt*
nutmeg

Line a straight-sided deep pie dish with shortcrust pastry. Prick over with a fork and leave for a while. Whisk the eggs well and add the sugar and salt. Add the milk and whisk thoroughly then strain into the pastry-lined dish. Grate a little nutmeg over the top of the custard and bake in a moderate oven for fifteen minutes, then in a very slow one for another twenty-five minutes until the custard is well set. Remove from the oven carefully and leave to go quite cold before serving. The custard should be well set and firm enough to cut with a knife to serve.

Dumplings

8 *oz. flour*	*a good pinch of salt*
1 *teaspoon baking powder*	1 *teacup or less of cold water*
4 *oz. shredded suet*	

Sift the flour with the baking powder and salt. Add the suet and mix well together. Moisten with just enough water to make a light dough. Pinch off pieces the size of a small egg and roll with floured hands. Drop into a pan of boiling stock or plain water and cook for twenty minutes. The dumplings may be served with braised or boiled beef, or as a sweet with syrup, jam or wine sauce (p. 32)

Fruit Flan

Quantities for an eight-inch flan:

1–1½ *lb. fruit*	1 *teaspoon arrowroot or* ¼ *oz.*
4 *oz. flan pastry (p.* 165)	*gelatine*
	thick whipped cream

Any stewed fruit, fresh or bottled, may be used. Cherries are particularly good. Prepare a flan case with flan pastry (p. 165), and bake in a hot oven for fifteen to twenty minutes until the pastry is cooked. Fill the flan case with sweetened fruit free of juice. Make a glaze with one teaspoon of arrowroot, or quarter of an ounce of gelatine, to quarter of a pint of fruit juice and when beginning to set, pour over the fruit. When quite cold, pile some thick whipped cream on the top and it is ready to serve.

Fruits, Stewed

Most fruits grown in England may be stewed either in a heavy saucepan on top of the stove or in a covered earthenware casserole in a slow oven. I prefer the latter method unless time is short as it retains the full flavour of the fruit. It is usually necessary to add a little water to any fruit but it depends on whether the fruit is very juicy or not and how much syrup is required, as to how much water should be used.

Granulated sugar or soft brown sugar, dark or light, may be used and here again the amount must be determined by the fruit used. When stewing rhubarb, I cut it into chunks, add half a cup of water, soft brown sugar and a pinch of salt and cook it in the oven, testing for sweetness when the fruit is soft. For those who do not care for plain stewed rhubarb, it is made more palatable by putting it through an electric blender when cooked and cooled, with the addition of a teaspoon of powdered gelatine and some thick cream. It makes a sweet which few will refuse.

Dried fruit should be washed first and soaked well overnight then cooked in the same water.

Ginger Pudding

8 oz. suet	1 tablespoon ground ginger
8 oz. flour	pinch of salt
8 oz. moist brown sugar	

Free the suet from skin and shred it as finely as possible. Sieve the flour with the ground ginger and mix together with the suet and sugar. Put the mixture, dry, into a buttered pudding basin, cover with a round of buttered foil or greaseproof paper and tie down with a pudding cloth. Boil for three hours or the equivalent in a pressure cooker. Serve with fresh cream or custard sauce (p. 22).

Gooseberry Fool

  1 *lb. ripe gooseberries* $\frac{1}{2}$ *pint thick cream* or *custard*
  $\frac{1}{2}$ *teacup water*   *(p. 22)*
  4 *oz. sugar*

Top and tail the gooseberries and put them in an earthenware
jar with the water and either stand the jar in a pan of boiling
water or place in a moderate oven until the fruit is soft and
tender, about fifteen to twenty minutes. Work the fruit through
a coarse sieve and put it back in the jar with the sugar. When the
sugar has melted, allow the fruit to cool a little and whisk in
the cream or custard. Spoon into a glass serving-dish or small
custard glasses and serve cold. Any soft fruit in season will
make a good fool.

Gooseberry Pudding

  $\frac{3}{4}$ *lb. suet crust (p.* 168)   4 *oz. moist brown sugar*
  1$\frac{1}{2}$ *lb. gooseberries*   *salt*

Line a buttered pudding basin with the thinly rolled suet crust,
leaving enough to cover the top of the pudding. Top and tail
the gooseberries and fill the basin, adding the sugar and a pinch
of salt. If the gooseberries are ripe and full of juice, water should
not be necessary, but if there is any doubt, one tablespoon of
cold water may be added.

Damp the edges of the suet crust before putting on the lid,
pinch well together to seal in the juice and cover with foil. Tie
on a cloth and put into a pan of boiling water. Boil for two or
three hours, or in a pressure cooker for the required time.
Remember to put a tablespoon of vinegar in the boiling
water.

Serve with a jug of fresh cream or custard sauce (p. 22).

Ice-Cream

This is a basic ice-cream mixture but flavouring such as coffee, chocolate or a teacup of any pulped stewed fruit may be added. If the fruit used is sour, add extra sugar.

1 *teacup caster sugar*	1 *teaspoon vanilla essence*
2 *teacups scalded milk*	1 *teacup double cream*
2–3 *eggs*	*pinch of salt*

Dissolve the sugar in the warmed milk, with the salt and vanilla essence. Separate the yolks from the whites of the eggs and beat the yolks into the mixture. Cook in a double saucepan or stir in a bowl over a pan of boiling water until thick. If fruit pulp is used, add at this stage and adjust sugar. Allow to cool while beating the egg whites stiffly. Fold in the egg whites and cream and freeze for three or four hours. If the ice-cream is made in the ice compartment of the refrigerator, it will be necessary to stir the mixture several times in order to prevent the formation of crystals.

Jam Tart

6 *oz. shortcrust pastry (p.* 167)	½ *lb. raspberry or plum jam*

Line a buttered pie plate with some shortcrust pastry, remembering to prick the bottom and let it rest to prevent the pastry from rising during cooking. Trim and decorate the edge, spread half a pound of jam over the pastry, decorate with twisted strips of pastry and bake in a hot oven for fifteen or twenty minutes. It may be eaten hot or cold.

Any jam may be used, but raspberry or plum jam are particularly suitable.

Junket

2 *pints new milk*	1 *dessertspoon rennet*
1 *tablespoon brandy* or ½ *pint*	½ *pint thick cream* (*if liked*)
white wine (*optional*)	*powdered cinnamon* or *nutmeg*
2 *oz. sugar*	

Warm the milk to blood heat and stir in the brandy, sugar and rennet. Pour into a glass serving-dish, cover and put in a cool place to set. Before serving, cover the junket with lightly whipped or clotted cream. Grate a little nutmeg over the top or sprinkle with cinnamon and caster sugar.

Lemon Meringue Pie

grated rind of 1 *lemon*	4 *oz. caster sugar*
6 *heaped teaspoons cornflour*	*juice of two or three lemons*
¼ *pint hot water*	3 *eggs*
a pinch of salt	8 *oz. flan pastry* (*p.* 165)
¼ *teaspoon cream of tartar*	3 *dessertspoons icing sugar*

Put the lemon rind, cornflour, sugar and water with a pinch of salt into the top of a double boiler or a bowl over a pan of simmering water. Stir until the sugar has dissolved and the mixture has thickened. Separate the egg yolks from the whites, mix the egg yolks with the lemon juice and add to the mixture. Simmer for ten or fifteen minutes.

Line a tart plate with the pastry and bake as in the recipe on p. 165. When the mixture has cooled a little, fill the pastry. Beat the egg white with the cream of tarter and three level dessertspoons of icing sugar until stiff and glossy. Spread over the pie and bake in a moderate oven until the meringue has browned.

Lemon Mousse

6 *eggs*	*salt*
4 *tablespoons caster sugar*	2 *tablespoons cold water*
juice and rind of 1 *or* 2 *lemons*	1 *level tablespoon gelatine*

Separate the egg yolks and whites into two bowls. Beat the sugar into the yolks with the finely grated lemon rind and a pinch of salt until thick and creamy. Meanwhile measure the water into a small saucepan and sprinkle in the gelatine. Let it soak until all the water is absorbed then stir in the lemon juice and put over a very low fire to dissolve the gelatine. Take care not to overheat or the gelatine will not set, and do not let it get too cold before stirring into the egg mixture or it will set too quickly and result in a lumpy mess. Fold in the stiffly beaten egg whites with a metal spoon and leave in a cold place to set. Before serving, pour some thick cream over the top and decorate with crystallized violets.

Tangerines or oranges make a change and I have frequently used all three fruits together.

Lemon Pudding

$\frac{3}{4}$ *lb. suet crust* (*p.* 168)	3 *lemons*
6 *oz. moist brown sugar*	*water*

Line a pudding basin with thinly rolled suet crust, leaving enough to make a lid for the top. Choose fresh juicy lemons and put them whole into the lined basin. Add the sugar with a pinch of salt and cover with water. Put on the lid, seal well by wetting the edges and pinch them together. Cover with buttered greaseproof paper, foil and a clean pudding cloth. Tie down and boil for at least three hours.

Meringues

Egg whites and sugar are the basic ingredients required for making meringues, though a little colouring or flavouring may be added if liked. The eggs should be fresh and at room temperature for the whites to whisk correctly. The temperature of the oven is important (not more than 200° F) and the meringues should be baked for two hours or more until they are crisp and dry. They will keep for several weeks if kept in a dry airy place but not in a tightly covered tin.

5 *egg whites*	¼ *teaspoon salt*
¼ *teaspoon cream of tartar*	8 *oz. caster sugar*

Prepare a baking-sheet by placing a sheet of lightly oiled greaseproof paper over it, oiled side uppermost. Separate the yolks from the whites of the eggs (taking care not to break the yolks if they are to be kept for later use). Whisk the egg whites very stiffly, gradually adding the cream of tartar, salt and four ounces of the sugar, a tablespoon at a time and beating continuously. The meringue should be stiff enough to hold its shape when formed. Gently fold in the rest of the sugar with a palette knife.

To make oval meringues, use a wetted tablespoon and a knife; for fancy shapes, a forcing bag and a plain nozzle. Place the meringues on the prepared baking-sheet on the bottom shelf of a cool oven and leave them for at least two hours until they are dry and crisp. Add some whipped cream filling and press two halves together.

Mince Pies

Mince pies are part of the traditional Christmas fare in Britain and the original mincemeat, as the name suggests, included lean cooked beef. Today this is invariably omitted although in America it is still quite often included.

shortcrust (p. 167) or flaky   *mincemeat (p. 232)*
   pastry (p. 164)   *1 egg white*

A rich shortcrust or flaky pastry are both good for mince pies. Roll out the pastry rather thinly and cut into rounds with a pastry cutter or a glass tumbler the size of your pastry tins. Line the buttered pastry tins with these rounds of pastry and put a good teaspoon of mincemeat in each. Gather the trimmings of pastry together and roll out. Cut out slightly smaller rounds this time and moisten the edges. Lay these rounds over the mincemeat and press the edges together lightly. Make a small gash in the top of each pie, brush over with white of egg and bake in a hot oven for twenty minutes, when the pastry should be cooked.

Mince pies may be eaten hot or cold. Dredge with fine sugar before serving.

Pancakes

Pancakes, to be successful, must be made with very fresh eggs. They are also improved if the egg yolks and whites are beaten and added separately and some old recipe books advocate the addition of a tablespoon of clean snow when possible. There are cooks who fill a dish with rolled and sugared pancakes before serving them but served in this manner they become limp and leathery. Pancakes are at their best served individually and sent to table quickly as soon as they come from the pan, crisp and hot.

4 oz. flour   *1 teaspoon olive oil*
½ teaspoon salt   *1 dessertspoon cold water*
1 egg   *lard*
½ pint milk

Sieve the flour and salt into a bowl. Make a well in the centre and break in the egg yolk. Use a wooden spoon to stir in the flour, add the milk slowly and beat for five minutes. Just before using, beat in the ice cold water and olive oil and fold in the well-beaten egg white.

Melt a small knob of lard in a heavy frying-pan and when it is smoking hot, pour in just enough batter to cover the bottom of the pan. Cook for one minute until the underside is golden brown, then toss or turn the pancake and cook the other side until crisp and golden. As the pancake cooks, shake the pan gently from time to time to prevent burning and to ensure even cooking. Roll the pancake on to a hot plate, dredge with fine sugar and serve at once with caster sugar, lemon juice or jam.

Plum Custard

1 *lb. ripe yellow plums*	3 *eggs*
2 *oz. sugar*	½ *pint milk*
water	*almond essence*

Remove the stones from the fruit carefully, damaging the fruit as little as possible, and put into a well-buttered baking-dish. Make a thick syrup with three tablespoons of the sugar and a little water, pour it over the plums and place in a moderate oven to cook. Separate the egg yolks from the whites and make a thick custard with the yolks, the remainder of the sugar and the milk. Put into a double boiler and cook until the custard coats the spoon. Stir in a few drops of almond essence, remove from the fire and cool. Whisk the egg white stiffly until it forms peaks and fold into the cooled custard with a metal spoon. Pile the mixture on top of the cold cooked plums and decorate with tiny macaroons, sometimes called ratafia biscuits.

Queen of Puddings

1 *pint milk*	1 *lemon*
2 *oz. butter*	4 *oz. caster sugar*
4 *oz. fine breadcrumbs*	*salt*
3 *eggs*	1 *dessertspoon icing sugar*

Warm the milk together with the butter and pour over the breadcrumbs. Add three ounces of sugar, a pinch of salt and the grated rind of a lemon and allow to cool. Separate the egg yolks from the whites and stir the beaten yolks into the mixture. Pour into a buttered pudding dish, let it stand for half an hour, then bake in a moderate oven for twenty minutes or more until the pudding has set. Beat the egg whites until stiff and fold in the rest of the sugar. Pile the meringue on top of the pudding, sprinkle with a little icing sugar and return to the oven for about ten minutes until the meringue is crisp and golden. Serve hot from the oven. Often a layer of apricot, strawberry or raspberry jam is spread thickly over the pudding before piling the meringue on top.

Red Currant and Raspberry Pie

1 *lb. red currants*
½ *lb. raspberries*
3 *heaped tablespoons sugar*

6 *oz. shortcrust pastry (p.*
167)

Strip the currants from the stalks and put them into a deep pie dish with a pie funnel or an egg cup, bottom upwards, placed in their midst. Add the raspberries and sprinkle in the sugar. Place a border of pastry round the edge of the dish, cover with the rest of the pastry and bake in a moderate oven one hour or less. Sift some fine sugar over the top before serving either hot or cold with custard (p. 22) or fresh cream.

Rice Pudding

2 *oz. round rice*
1 *oz. sugar*
1½ *pints milk*

nutmeg
salt
butter or *beef suet*

Wash the rice and put it into an earthenware baking-dish with the salt, sugar and milk. Stir and add a good knob of suet or butter. Grate some nutmeg on the top and bake in a slow oven for about two hours. The rice should absorb all the milk and long slow cooking gives a creamy pudding.

Serve hot or cold.

Roly Poly Jam Pudding

Sometimes called Shirt Sleeve Pudding, as an old shirt sleeve was often kept and used for boiling the pudding.

¾ lb. suet crust (p. 168)   *black currant jam*

Roll out the suet crust to a thickness of about a quarter of an inch. Spread the jam evenly over it, leaving a small margin round the edges. Roll up tightly, pinch the ends to keep the jam from running out and tie in a floured cloth, allowing room for the pudding to swell. Put the pudding into boiling salted water and boil for two hours.

Sago or Tapioca Pudding

1½ pints milk	*butter*
3 oz. sago or *tapioca*	*nutmeg*
3 oz. sugar	

Put the sago, or tapioca, with the sugar into an earthenware oven dish. Stir in the milk, add a knob of butter and grate some nutmeg over the top. Place in a slow oven for up to two hours until the pudding is thick and creamy and a brown skin has formed on the top.

Spotted Dick

8 oz. flour	*½ teaspoon bicarbonate of soda*
4 oz. suet	*½ teaspoon cream of tartar*
3 oz. sugar	*salt*
4 oz. currants	*milk*

Sieve the flour, salt, cream of tartar and soda together and add the finely chopped suet, sugar and cleaned currants. Mix well with enough milk to make a soft dough and press into a well-buttered pudding basin. Cover with oiled greaseproof paper or foil, tie down with a clean pudding cloth and boil for three hours. Serve with custard sauce (p. 22).

Summer Pudding

There are several ways of making this pudding according to the fruit available and the will of the cook. Some butter the thinly sliced bread, others do not. It may be made from fruit stewed whole or sieved which many prefer if the fruit used has many seeds. If raspberries are used alone, there is no need to stew them if they are ripe. Just sprinkle caster sugar over each layer of fruit to bring out the juice.

thin slices of white bread	*2 or 3 oz. sugar*
butter	*pinch of salt*
2 lb. fruit (see recipe)	*½ pint water*

Cut off the crusts of some thin slices of bread and butter and line a pudding basin or soufflé dish with the butter side to the basin. Stew about two pounds of fruit—red currants, black currants, blackberries and apple mixed together or fresh raspberries. Damsons are also frequently used. Add two or three ounces of sugar, a pinch of salt and half a pint of water. It is difficult to give exact amounts; it depends on the ripeness of the fruit used. While the fruit is still hot, spoon some fruit into the basin with enough juice to soak the bottom layer of bread. Cover with a thin slice of unbuttered bread, more fruit and juice finishing with a final layer of bread. Put a plate which just fits inside the top of the basin and place a heavy weight on the plate so that the juice is pressed into the bread. Leave for twenty-four hours in a cold larder or refrigerator. To serve, turn the pudding out on to a dish and cover with whipped cream. If properly made there should be no trace of white bread showing.

Syllabub (1)

In the days when it was fashionable to be plump and a man's importance in the world was judged by the size of his corporation, syllabubs were made with lots of sugar and sweet wine. Nowadays, when slimness counts, we reduce the amount of sugar and lace the wine with brandy. There are many variations of syllabub, but the following are the ones I like best.

1 *pint thick cream*	2 *lemons*
2 *oz. caster sugar*	1 *tablespoon brandy*
1 *gill sweetish sherry* or *white wine*	*salt*

If the syllabub is to be eaten the same day, mix the cream together with the sugar, white wine or sherry, the juice of both lemons and the finely grated peel of one. Add the brandy and a pinch of salt and whisk until the mixture is quite thick and stands in soft peaks. Pour into individual glasses and serve chilled.

If, however, the syllabub is to be kept, bring the cream to the boil, let it stand until cold, then proceed as above. This should keep up to three days.

Syllabub (2)

½ *pint sweet white wine*	*sugar to taste*
½ *glass brandy*	1 *pint thick cream*
juice of half a lemon	*salt*

Put the wine, brandy and lemon juice into a bowl, add sugar to taste, a pinch of salt and the cream. Whip all together until very thick and serve very cold in tall glasses. An electric blender makes an excellent syllabub very quickly.

Syllabub (3)

6 *egg yolks*

6 *tablespoons Madeira* or *Marsala*

3 *tablespoons caster sugar*

salt

Put the egg yolks into a basin with the wine, sugar and a pinch of salt. Beat until all are well combined. Have ready a pan of water just off the boil and place the basin in it, or pour the contents of the basin into the top of a double saucepan. Keep the water at the same temperature over a low fire and whisk the mixture to a smooth, stiff froth. Remove from the fire and continue beating for a minute or the eggs may curdle. Pour into individual glasses and serve warm or cold.

Syrup Pudding

8 *oz. self-raising flour*

4 *oz. suet*

pinch of salt

water

golden syrup

Make a suet crust with eight ounces of self-raising flour, four ounces of finely chopped suet, a good pinch of salt, and water to mix (for method see p. 168).

Put a good tablespoon of golden syrup at the bottom of a well-buttered pudding basin. Press in the suet crust, cover with buttered paper or foil, tie on a pudding cloth and boil for at least two hours.

Turn the pudding out of the basin and serve with a sauce-boat of hot syrup.

Syrup Tart

6 *oz. shortcrust pastry (p.* 167)

3 *tablespoons breadcrumbs*

4 *tablespoons golden syrup*

1 *teaspoon lemon juice*

Line a buttered plate with the pastry. Trim and decorate the edges with a fork. Prick the pastry over with a fork and rest to prevent the pastry from rising in the middle when cooking. Spread the breadcrumbs thickly over the pastry, warm the lemon juice with the syrup and pour over the breadcrumbs covering them completely. Decorate the tart in a lattice pattern with strips of pastry and bake in a hot oven about twenty minutes when the pastry should be cooked.

It may be served hot or cold.

Trifle

26 *Savoy biscuits* or *a stale sponge cake*
½ *lb. raspberry jam*
2 *oz. ratafia biscuits*
1 *large wineglass sherry* or *Madeira*
1 *pint custard* (*p. 22*)
½ *pint double cream*
1 *oz. blanched almonds*
angelica, crystallized violets

Spread the jam thickly over the sponge cake or sandwich between the Savoy biscuits and arrange in a glass serving-dish. Spread a layer of ratafia biscuits and pour on the sherry or Madeira and leave to soak for half an hour. Allow the custard to cool a little before pouring into the dish and leave to set. Whip the cream but not too stiffly and spread over the top of the trifle. Decorate with the blanched and split almonds stuck into the cream endwise, a shred or two of angelica and a few crystallized violets.

12. Bread, Cakes and Biscuits

Baking day, usually Friday, is still the day of the week reserved for the making of pastry, cakes, biscuits and, more rarely these days, bread. North countrywomen, Cornish women and the Welsh bake in batches to last over the week-end and through the following week until baking day comes round again. The amount of cakes consumed in Great Britain is astonishing, even among those who no longer bake at home. To have 'no cake in the house' is an admonishment of the lazy housewife by the industrious and is deplored in many parts of the country even today.

BREAD, BUNS AND SCONES

Bread

To eat 'bought bread' was a stigma which brought frowns of disapproval to the brows of my mother's elders when I was a child. For most of us the days of baking our own bread in big batches has gone for good but alas the bread bought in shops so little resembles home baking that for those who would like to enjoy the pleasures of a homemade loaf a recipe is included. Bread is not difficult to make but it does take time and one must be sure to make it in a warm even temperature, free from draughts. Bread dough catches cold very easily and if it does, it does not rise well and the bread will be heavy and leaden.

1 *oz. yeast*	3½ *lb. plain flour*
1 *teaspoon sugar*	½ *oz. salt*
warm water	

Break up the yeast, mix it in a basin with the sugar and half a pint of warm water, and let it stand until it becomes frothy. Put the flour and salt into a large mixing bowl, draw some of it to the sides of the bowl, leaving a hole in the centre. Pour in the yeast, sprinkle the top with flour, cover it with a clean cloth, and let it rest in a warm place for twenty-five minutes.

Using both hands, flip some more flour on to the yeast and mix with the flour to a soft but not sticky dough. When the dough is formed knead it well for at least ten minutes. The more the dough is slapped and pummelled the finer the bread will be. Cover once more with a clean damp cloth and let it stand—still in a warm place—to prove for one hour or until the dough has doubled in size.

Cut off pieces of dough and form into loaves or fit into well-greased tins and again leave to rise for fifteen minutes. If there is any dough left over, form it into rolls, prod a hole in the middle and remember to flour the baking sheet on which they will bake. Put the bread into a pre-heated moderately hot oven and bake for ten minutes, then reduce the heat. Cook for forty-five to sixty minutes in all depending on the size of the loaves.

Remove the bread from the oven, turn the loaves out of the tins gently and knock the bottom of each loaf with the knuckles when it should sound hollow. Stand the loaves on a rack out of all draughts to cool.

Bath Buns

8 *oz. flour*	3 *oz. butter*
a pinch of salt	⅛ *pint milk*

½ oz. yeast

1 beaten egg

2 oz. caster sugar

2 oz. sultanas

1 oz. candied peel

egg and milk to glaze

1 oz. loaf sugar

Sieve the flour and salt and rub in the butter. Warm the milk and use a little of it to cream the yeast. Pour yeast and milk into the flour, add the egg and beat very thoroughly, cover with a cloth and leave to rise in a warm place until it doubles its size. This will take an hour and a half. Add sugar and fruit, beat well once again and form into small balls. Put them on a well-greased baking sheet and leave them to prove to double their size. Brush with a little egg and milk to glaze and sprinkle with crushed loaf sugar. Bake in a hot oven for twenty or thirty minutes.

Potato Cakes

1 lb. potatoes

1 teaspoon salt

1 oz. butter

3 oz. flour

Choose floury potatoes and boil, drain and sieve them. Add the softened butter and salt and work in the flour. Knead lightly to a soft dough and turn on to a floured board. Roll the dough out to a thickness of about a quarter of an inch, cut into triangles and cook in a hot, greased heavy frying pan until brown on both sides. Serve hot with plenty of butter.

Scones

The following is a plain scone mixture but any dried fruits may be added for variety.

8 oz. flour

1 level teaspoon bicarbonate of
    soda

2 level teaspoons cream of
    tartar

½ teaspoon salt

2 oz. butter or lard

¼ pint milk or butter-milk

Sieve the flour with the soda, cream of tartar and salt. Rub in the butter and add dried fruit if used. Mix with the milk to a very soft dough and turn on to a floured board. Press out to a thickness of half an inch and cut into rounds or triangles. Place on an ungreased, floured baking-sheet and bake for ten or fifteen minutes in a hot oven.

Scotch Pancakes (Drop Scones)

8 oz. flour	salt
½ teaspoon bicarbonate of soda	1 egg
1 teaspoon cream of tartar	½ pint milk
1 dessertspoon sugar or syrup	

Sieve the flour with the bicarbonate of soda and cream of tartar into a bowl. Make a well in the centre of the flour and add the sugar or syrup, whichever is used, a pinch of salt and break in the unbeaten egg. Beat to a stiff batter adding the milk a little at a time. Drop a teaspoonful at a time, well spaced, on a hot, greased griddle or a large frying-pan. Let the pancakes brown on one side, then turn them over and brown on the other side. Spread with butter to serve.

Singing Hinnies

1 lb. plain flour	½ teaspoon cream of tartar
4 oz. lard	½ teaspoon bicarbonate of soda
4 oz. butter	6 oz. currants
½ teaspoon salt	milk

Sieve the flour with the salt and rising agents, rub in the butter and lard and add the currants. Use as much milk as is necessary to form a soft but firm dough. Shape it into a round like a muffin and roll out to a quarter of an inch thick, grease a baking-sheet or a griddle if you have one; prick the cake all over with a fork and put into a moderately hot oven and cook until the underside is brown, about five to seven minutes. Turn it over with a palette knife and cook the other side until brown. Cut into convenient pieces, split them while hot, butter them generously and serve quickly.

CAKES

Almond Cake

4 oz. butter	2 oz. ground almonds
4 oz. sugar	½ teaspoon baking powder
2 eggs	salt
4 oz. flour	

Cream the butter and sugar together and add the well-beaten eggs. Sieve the flour three times with the baking powder and a good pinch of salt and add to the creamed mixture together with the ground almonds. Pour into a prepared cake tin and bake in a moderate oven for about one hour until well risen and golden. This cake should be moist and is better if kept a day or two in an airtight cake tin.

Cherry Cake

8 oz. flour	6 oz. butter
¼ teaspoon salt	6 oz. sugar
½ teaspoon baking powder	3 eggs
3 oz. glacé cherries	milk

Sieve the flour, salt and baking powder and add the cherries cut into quarters. Cream the butter and sugar together and beat in the eggs one at a time. Fold in the dry ingredients and add a little milk if necessary. Put into a prepared cake tin, sprinkle with caster sugar and bake in a moderate oven for about one hour.

Chocolate Cake (uncooked)

4 oz. butter
1 tablespoon syrup
3 tablespoons drinking chocolate
½ lb. Marie biscuits
1 tablespoon brandy
4 oz. milk chocolate

Melt the butter, syrup and chocolate in a basin over fast-boiling water. Break the biscuits into small pieces and add to the cooled mixture. Stir in the brandy until well mixed and turn into a greased loose-bottomed cake tin. Press well down and when quite cold, cover with melted chocolate.

Christmas Cake

Because of its richness, Christmas cake should be made three or four weeks beforehand and kept in an airtight tin to keep it moist. A few days before it is needed, it may be covered with almond paste (p. 218) and when that is set, iced and decorated with royal icing (p. 219).

The amounts and cooking time given below make a large cake to be cooked in a tin 9″ × 3¾″; if a smaller cake is required, use half the quantities and bake in a tin 7½″ × 3″ for three hours. The combination of honey and brandy help in keeping the cake moist.

12 oz. butter
8 oz. brown sugar
4 oz. honey
6 eggs
1 lb. flour
½ teaspoon salt
1 lb. sultanas
1 lb. currants
4 oz. raisins
6 oz. candied peel
2 oz. glacé cherries
4 oz. chopped almonds
1 teaspoon allspice
2 tablespoons treacle
1 wineglass brandy
almond paste
royal icing

204

Clean the fruit and mix in the brandy. Beat the butter and sugar to a cream and add each egg separately, beating until the mixture is stiff and uniform. Stir in the sifted flour, salt, fruit, chopped almonds, spice, treacle and brandy. Mix well, then transfer to a tin lined with greased paper and bake in a slow oven for six hours and twenty minutes. If the top of the cake is becoming too brown, cut a piece of greaseproof paper or foil the size of the tin and lay it on top of the cake.

Doughnuts

8 oz. flour
pinch of salt
2 oz. butter
½ oz. yeast
caster sugar

3–4 tablespoons warmed milk
1 beaten egg
ground cinnamon (if liked)
oil for frying

Warm the sieved salt and flour in a basin and rub in the butter. Cream the yeast with one teaspoon of sugar and add the milk and beaten egg. Pour into the flour and mix to a soft dough. Beat well with a wooden spoon or your hand and leave to rise in a warm place until the dough has doubled its size. Knead lightly and divide into ten or twelve pieces. Shape each piece into a ball and flatten with the palm of your hand. Put half a teaspoon of jam in the centre and gather the edges together over the jam. Place the doughnuts on a well-oiled and floured baking-sheet and leave in a warm place to prove—about six or seven minutes. Heat the oil in a deep pan and when it is slightly smoking, put in the doughnuts, a few at a time until they are golden brown and cooked through. This should take five minutes. Lift them carefully from the pan and place on kitchen paper and dredge with caster sugar or sugar and cinnamon. Serve fresh and still warm.

Dundee Cake

6 oz. sultanas	½ teaspoon baking powder
3 oz. currants	6 oz. butter
3 oz. candied peel	6 oz. sugar
3 oz. blanched almonds	3 eggs
9 oz. flour	milk
¼ teaspoon salt	

Clean and dry the currants and sultanas and slice the peel finely. Chop the almonds keeping a few aside for the top of the cake. Sieve the flour together with the salt and baking powder. Cream the butter and sugar and beat in the eggs one at a time. Add the dry ingredients and moisten with a little milk if necessary. The mixture should be rather stiff. Put it into a prepared cake tin and press the halved almonds on the top. Bake in a moderate oven for about two hours reducing to a lower heat for the second hour.

Easter Cake

4 oz. currants	8 oz. flour
4 oz. raisins	salt
1 oz. chopped peel	¼ teaspoon ginger
4 oz. butter	¼ teaspoon cinnamon
4 oz. brown sugar	¼ teaspoon grated nutmeg
2–3 eggs	milk
1 teaspoon grated lemon peel	almond paste (p. 218)
1 teaspoon grated orange peel	beaten egg
1 level teaspoon baking powder	

Clean and dry the fruit and add the chopped peel. Cream the butter and sugar until soft and fluffy and add the beaten eggs a little at a time. Next put in the grated orange and lemon peel, fold in the sieved flour, a good pinch of salt, spices and baking powder. Add enough milk to give a soft dropping consistency and fold in the cleaned fruit. Place half the mixture in an oiled and lined cake tin and put on it a thin layer of almond paste. Add the rest of the cake mixture and bake in a moderate oven for about two and a half hours. When the cake is cold decorate it round the edges with small balls of almond paste to represent easter eggs, brush them with a little beaten egg, and brown in the top of a hot oven or under the grill but take care the almond paste does not burn.

Eccles Cakes

4 *oz. currants*	*salt*
2 *oz. soft brown sugar*	8 *oz. flaky pastry (p.* 164)
2 *oz. butter*	*caster sugar*
1 *oz. chopped candied peel*	

Scald the currants and mix with the brown sugar, butter, peel and a pinch of salt. Roll out the pastry one-eighth of an inch thick and cut into circles four inches across. Put a dessertspoonful of the mixture on each circle. Gather up the edges and seal well. Turn the cakes over and roll lightly until the currants just show. Make two small slits in each cake, brush with water and sprinkle with caster sugar. Bake in a hot oven for twenty minutes.

Fruit Cake

8 *oz. butter*	1 *oz. currants*
10 *oz. flour*	1 *oz. raisins*
8 *oz. sugar*	2 *eggs*
1 *tablespoon ground almonds*	1 *dessertspoon syrup*
1 *teaspoon mixed spice*	*almond essence*
salt	*milk*

Rub the butter into the flour and add the sugar, ground

almonds, mixed spice, salt, currants and raisins. Mix well before adding the beaten eggs, syrup, a few drops of almond essence and if necessary a little milk, to give a stiff dropping consistency. Put the mixture into a prepared roasting-tin, decorate the top with a few split almonds, and bake in a moderate oven for one and a quarter hours.

Gingerbread

This is Eliza Acton's recipe for gingerbread as she gave it in 1845 (*Modern Cookery for Private Families*). I use golden syrup instead of treacle and reduce the amount to one pound but otherwise follow the recipe as given. The gingerbread should be kept at least a week before it is eaten.

5 *eggs*	1 *lb. flour*
1¼ *lb. treacle*	1 *oz. ground ginger*
6 *oz. moist brown sugar*	2 *lemons*
6 *oz. butter*	*salt*

Beat the eggs to a froth and slowly add the warmed treacle or syrup beating all the time. Add the sugar in the same manner and then the butter previously warmed and softened but not melted. Sift the flour, ginger and a good pinch of salt together and add slowly to the other ingredients beating constantly until bubbles appear on the surface. Grate in the rind of the lemons and turn into a buttered roasting-tin. Bake for two hours in a slow oven.

Ginger Cake

1 *lb. flour*	½ *lb. butter*
1 *teaspoon baking powder*	6 *oz. sugar*
salt	1 *teacup syrup*
1 *dessertspoon ground ginger*	1 *teacup boiling water*

Sift the flour, baking powder, salt and ginger together in a mixing-bowl and rub in the butter with the fingertips. Add the sugar, warmed syrup and at the last moment a teacup of boiling water. Stir well and pour into a well-buttered roasting-tin. Bake in a moderate oven for about one hour and do not open the oven door for at least half an hour. Test by inserting a metal skewer into the cake and, if it comes out clean, the cake is done.

Lardy Cake

2 *lb. white bread dough* (*p. 199*)	1 *oz. caraway seeds* or 4 *oz. currants*
6 *oz. butter* or *lard*	2 *oz. sugar*
7 *oz. sugar*	3 *tablespoons water*

Roll out the dough into an oblong and spread on it half the butter and half the sugar covering only the top two-thirds of the dough. Sprinkle the caraway seeds or currants over the butter and sugar. Fold the dough into three portions bringing the bottom third up first and folding the top third over it. Seal the ends by pressing them with the rolling-pin and half-turn the dough. Roll out again into an oblong, spread the top two-thirds with the remaining butter and sugar, fold and turn as before, rolling out to fit into a Yorkshire pudding tin. The dough should be one to one and a half inches thick. Leave it to rise in a warm place away from draughts and bake in a moderately hot oven about one hour. When half-cooked the cake may be brushed with a thick sugar-and-water syrup. To make the syrup, dissolve two ounces of sugar in three table-spoons of water and bring to the boil. It should take about four or five minutes to boil until it is thick and syrupy.

Maids of Honour

8 oz. shortcrust or flaky   2 oz. caster sugar
   pastry (pp. 167 and 164)   2 oz. ground almonds
2 eggs   raspberry jam

Use either shortcrust or flaky pastry to line some buttered patty tins. Beat the eggs with the sugar until creamy and add the ground almonds. Put half a teaspoon of raspberry jam in the centre of each lined patty tin and cover with one teaspoon of ground almonds and egg mixture. Decorate with strips of pastry in the form of a cross and bake in a moderately hot oven for fifteen minutes.

Mrs. Boast's Cake

4 oz. butter   8 oz. currants
4 oz. caster sugar   8 oz. sultanas
8 oz. flour   2 oz. glacé cherries
½ teaspoon baking powder   a few peeled and split almonds
pinch of salt   for the top
2 or 3 eggs

Cream the butter and sugar until light and fluffy. Add the lightly beaten eggs, a little at a time alternating with the sieved flour, baking powder and salt. Beat the mixture very thoroughly and add the fruit. The cherries should be chopped fine. Line a seven-inch cake tin with oiled greaseproof paper, put in the mixture, put the almonds on top and lay a piece of greaseproof paper on top of the cake. Bake in the centre of a moderately hot oven for one hour then turn down to slow for the second hour. If you need to open the oven door while the cake is baking, do so in the last half hour or the fruit may sink to the bottom of the cake.

Orange Cake

5 oz. butter	½ teaspoon baking powder
6 oz. sugar	¼ teaspoon salt
1 large orange	a little milk if mixture is too
2–3 eggs	stiff
6 oz. flour	

Cream the butter and sugar together until white. Add the grated peel and juice of the orange and beat in the eggs, one at a time. Sieve the flour, salt and baking powder together and beat into the mixture a little at a time. Put into a prepared cake tin and bake in a moderate oven for about three-quarters of an hour. Test by inserting a metal skewer into the cake. If it comes out clean, the cake is ready.

Parkin

A traditional Yorkshire cake eaten on Guy Fawkes Day. It should be kept in an airtight tin for at least two weeks before it is ready for eating.

1 lb. medium oatmeal	6 oz. butter
8 oz. flour	8 oz. moist brown sugar
1 teaspoon baking powder	1 lb. syrup
1 small lemon	1 teacup of milk
2 teaspoons powdered ginger	1 egg

Mix all the dry ingredients together in a large mixing-bowl. Warm the butter, sugar and syrup together and when they are mixed, add the lemon juice and stir into the dry ingredients. Moisten with milk and a well-beaten egg. Beat very well to ensure lightness and pour the mixture, which should be of a dropping consistency, into a well-buttered roasting-tin and place in a moderate oven for one hour; then reduce the heat and bake for one hour more in a slow oven. Test by inserting a clean metal skewer into the parkin. If it is cooked, the skewer will come out clean. When quite cold, cut the parkin into two pieces, place a piece of greaseproof paper between the two halves and put it into an airtight cake tin.

Queen Cakes

4 oz. butter	½ teaspoon baking powder
4 oz. sugar	2 oz. sultanas
2 eggs	salt
4 oz. flour	milk

Beat the butter and sugar to a cream and add the well-beaten eggs a little at a time and beat again until the mixture is almost white. Sieve the flour two or three times with a pinch of salt and the baking powder and fold carefully into the creamed butter and sugar. Add the sultanas, cleaned and rolled in flour. If necessary, add a little milk to give a soft dropping consistency. Fill some buttered patty tins and bake in a moderately hot oven for twenty minutes. Turn out on a wire rack to cool.

Rock Cakes

12 oz. flour	5 oz. sugar
pinch of salt	3 oz. currants
2 teaspoons baking powder	1½ oz. candied peel
¼ teaspoon grated nutmeg	1 egg
¼ teaspoon mixed spice	milk
6 oz. butter	

Sieve the flour with the salt, baking powder and spices and rub in the butter as if for pastry. Stir in the sugar, currants and peel and mix well. Beat the egg and pour it into a well, formed in the centre of the mixture. Add enough milk to make a stiff mixture. Have ready a well-oiled baking-sheet and with a teaspoon and fork make rocky heaps on the baking-sheet. Bake in a hot oven for fifteen to twenty minutes.

Seed Cake

4 oz. butter	1 teaspoon baking powder
4 oz. caster sugar	1 dessertspoon caraway seeds
3 eggs	salt
8 oz. flour	

Beat the butter and sugar to a cream. Add the well-beaten egg yolks and the sieved flour and baking powder. Whisk the egg whites to a stiff froth and fold into the mixture. Add the caraway seeds and pour into a prepared cake tin. Bake in a moderate oven for one and a half hours.

Simnel Cake

A traditional cake baked for Simnel Sunday, the fourth Sunday in Lent. To make, use the same amounts given for Easter cake (p. 206) and omit the almond paste for the top. Decorate with split whole almonds instead. Simnel cakes are not usually baked in cake tins but formed into round loaves. Cook on a baking-sheet in the centre of a moderately hot oven for about one hour.

Sly Cake

8 oz. flaky or shortcrust pastry (pp. 164 and 167)	candied peel (if liked)
3–4 oz. currants	2 oz. sugar
	rose-water

Roll out some flaky or shortcrust pastry into an oblong shape. Cover half the pastry with the cleaned currants and sugar. If liked, some chopped candied peel may also be added. Sprinkle with a little rose-water and fold over the remaining pastry.

Damp the edges, pinching them together, and lightly roll the pastry until the currants show through. Bake in a moderate oven for half an hour.

Sponge Sandwich

4 *eggs*	*salt*
3 *oz. caster sugar*	*jam*
2 *oz. flour*	*thick cream (if liked)*
1 *teaspoon baking powder*	

Whisk the eggs thoroughly and beat in the sugar little by little. Continue to beat until the mixture is white and thick. Sieve the flour and baking powder together with a pinch of salt and fold into the beaten eggs and sugar. Have ready two buttered and floured sandwich tins. Pour half the mixture into each tin and bake in the centre of a hot oven for fifteen or twenty minutes. After removing the cakes from the oven leave them to shrink a little before turning them out on a wire tray. Spread one half with jam, and if liked thick whipped cream, sandwich the two halves together and dredge with caster sugar. When in season, sliced fresh strawberries in place of the jam make a delicious change.

Treacle Loaf

2 *oz. butter*	8 *oz. self-raising flour*
½ *gill milk*	1 *teaspoon mixed spice*
2 *oz. soft brown sugar*	*salt*
2 *tablespoons black treacle*	1 *egg*
4 *oz. sultanas*	

Put the butter, milk, sugar, treacle and sultanas into a saucepan and warm them gently until soft and the butter and sugar have melted. Sift the flour into a bowl with the spice and a pinch of salt, make a well in the centre and break in the beaten egg. Add the cooled milk mixture and beat to a smooth paste. Turn into a greased pound loaf tin and bake in a moderate oven for three-quarters of an hour. To test if it is cooked insert a skewer and if it comes out clean the loaf is ready. Turn out of the tin and cool on a wire rack.

Serve thinly sliced and spread with farmhouse butter.

Victoria Sandwich Cake

This is a basic sandwich cake mixture and a variety of fillings provides different flavoured cakes. Add two tablespoons of extra strong coffee to the mixture instead of milk to make a coffee cake and two tablespoons of chocolate powder for a chocolate cake.

4 oz. butter	4 oz. self-raising flour
4 oz. sugar	salt
2 eggs	1 tablespoon milk

Cream the butter and sugar together and add the well-beaten eggs. Fold in the sifted flour and a pinch of salt and moisten with the milk. Pour the mixture into two prepared sandwich tins and bake in a moderate oven for half an hour. Turn out to cool on a cake rack. Spread with jam, lemon curd or a butter icing filling (p. 218). Dredge with fine sugar over the top or prepare a soft icing.

BISCUITS

Ginger Biscuits

3 oz. butter	1 teaspoon ground ginger
½ oz. sugar	¼ teaspoon baking powder
3 oz. syrup	salt
4 oz. flour	

Warm the butter, sugar and syrup together and sift in the flour, ginger and baking powder. Add a pinch of salt and knead into a dough. Form the dough into balls the size of a large walnut and space them on a greased baking-sheet. Flatten with the palm of the hand and bake in a very slow oven for about half an hour when the biscuits should be crisp and golden. Leave them to cool on a wire cake rack and keep in an airtight tin or they will become soft by absorbing moisture from the air.

Ginger Nuts

4 oz. flour	1 oz. sugar
1 teaspoon baking powder	2 oz. butter
1 teaspoon ground ginger	salt
2 tablespoons syrup	

Sieve the flour with the baking powder, salt and ginger into a bowl. Put the syrup, butter and sugar into a small saucepan over a low heat and when melted, add to the dry ingredients. Mix well with a wooden spoon until a firm paste has been formed. Pinch off small pieces and roll into balls the size of walnuts and put them on an oiled baking-sheet at least two inches apart. Flatten slightly with the palm of the hand and bake in a cool oven for twenty minutes.

Flapjacks

1 teacup flour	$\frac{1}{2}$ teaspoon bicarbonate of soda
1 teacup rolled oats	1 tablespoon syrup
1 teacup desiccated coconut	4 oz. butter
1 teacup sugar	1 tablespoon cold water
salt	

Mix the flour, oats and coconut together with the soda and add a pinch of salt. Melt the butter, sugar and syrup and add the dry ingredients. Mix well and add the cold water. Pour the mixture into a small buttered baking-tin and bake in a moderate hot oven until cooked. Allow to cool a little then cut into squares with a sharp knife. When quite cold, remove from the tin. Note: If desiccated coconut is not liked, put in two teacups of rolled oats.

Shortbread

Shortbread is usually associated with Scotland. The secret of successful shortbread is the complete blending of the ingredients in a warm atmosphere and very slow baking.

6 *oz. flour*	4 *oz. butter*
2 *oz. caster sugar*	*salt*

Sieve the flour into a warmed bowl with the salt, add the sugar and knead with the softened butter until well blended. Press into a flan tin and crimp the edges with the finger and thumb. Prick a design on the shortbread with a fork and bake in a slow oven for twenty-five to thirty minutes until firm and pale brown. Cool on a wire tray and dredge with caster sugar.

When the shortbread is cold, cut into wedge-shaped pieces with a sharp knife and keep in an airtight cake tin or it will absorb moisture from the atmosphere and become soft.

Shrewsbury Biscuits

4 *oz. butter*	8 *oz. flour*
4 *oz. sugar*	1 *lemon*
1 *egg*	*salt*

Cream the butter and sugar together and beat well. Add the whisked egg slowly and continue to beat. Add the sieved flour, a pinch of salt and the grated rind of the lemon. Mix to a stiff paste and turn on to a floured board. Knead lightly and roll out thinly. Cut into fancy shapes and place on a baking-sheet. Bake in a slow moderate oven for half an hour until lightly browned. Remove from the oven and cool on a wire cake rack.

Sweet Oat Biscuits

2 *oz. butter*	1 *teacup rolled oats*
2 *oz. lard*	1 *teaspoon syrup*
3 *oz. sugar*	3 *teaspoons boiling water*
4 *oz. flour*	½ *teaspoon baking powder*
salt	

Cream the butter, lard and sugar together and stir in the sieved flour, salt, baking powder and oats. Add the syrup and boiling water and mix all together to a stiff biscuit mixture. Drop one heaped teaspoonful at a time on to a greased baking-sheet and bake in a cool oven for about half an hour until crisp.

ICINGS

Almond Paste

8 *oz. ground almonds*	1 *egg*
8 *oz. Barbados sugar* or *caster sugar*	1 *tablespoon brandy* or *orange juice*

Mix the ground almonds with the sugar, add the brandy or orange juice, then stir in the beaten egg slowly. Knead well and use as required.

Butter Icing

2 *oz. butter*	1 *tablespoon orange* or *lemon juice*
4 *oz. icing sugar*	or 1 *dessertspoon coffee* or *chocolate powder*

Cream the butter with the sifted icing sugar. Add one tablespoon of orange or lemon juice or one dessertspoon coffee or chocolate powder. Use for sandwich cakes.

Glacé Icing

4 oz. icing sugar
*1 tablespoon lemon juice or 1 oz. chocolate dissolved
   in 1 tablespoon water*

Sift the icing sugar into a bowl. Add the lemon juice, or dissolve the chocolate in one tablespoon of water and add to the sugar. Beat well and use at once.

Royal Icing

1 lb. icing sugar   *2 teaspoons lemon juice*
2 egg whites   *½ teaspoon glycerine*

Sieve the icing sugar several times and put most of it into a bowl keeping some on one side in case the mixture is too soft. Make a well in the centre of the sugar and gradually stir in the lightly beaten egg whites. Beat in the lemon juice and glycerine and continue beating until the mixture is glossy and stiff enough not to run off the cake. Use a knife dipped in hot water to smooth the icing. To prevent the icing in the bowl from becoming too stiff cover it with a damp cloth.

13. Pickles

Few people have the time or energy to make their own pickles and preserves these days and rely on their grocer to provide them when they are wanted. Nevertheless, the home-made product is usually so superior that I make no excuse for including a few favourites for those who prefer to make their own.

Pickled Cabbage

1 *red cabbage*   *spiced vinegar (p. 225)*
salt

Choose a firm red cabbage and remove the outer leaves. Shred the heart finely and spread out on a large dish. Sprinkle generously with common salt, toss the cabbage with the hands to distribute the salt and leave covered for twenty-four hours. Drain the cabbage and pack into clean jars and cover with spiced vinegar. Cover closely and keep for one week before using. Pickled cabbage may be stored for three or four months after which it loses its crispness and colour and becomes soft and flabby.

Pickled Lemons

brine (1 *lb. common salt to*   6 *lemons*
1 *quart of water*)   *water*

1 *quart vinegar*	$\frac{1}{4}$ *oz. mace*
$\frac{1}{2}$ *oz. cloves*	$\frac{1}{4}$ *oz. chillies*
$\frac{1}{2}$ *oz. white pepper*	$\frac{1}{2}$ *oz. mustard seed*
1 *oz. bruised ginger*	4 *cloves garlic*

Choose sound thick skinned lemons of equal size and put them into a brine of one pound of common salt to a quart of water. Let them stay in the brine for six days giving them a stir each day. On the sixth day remove from the brine and put them in a saucepan. Cover with boiling water and boil for fifteen minutes when they should be soft and tender. Take them from the water and leave them to go cold and quite dry before putting them into a stone jar. Boil the spices in the vinegar for half an hour and while still boiling, strain the vinegar over the lemons. When cold, seal carefully and keep for twelve months before using.

Mint Jelly

6 *lb. green apples*	*sugar*
large bunch of fresh mint	*water*
4 *lemons*	*green colouring*

Wash but do not core or peel the apples; cut them into pieces and put them into a preserving-pan with a few sprigs of mint and barely cover with water. Bring to the boil, add the juice of the lemons and simmer until the apples have fallen. Strain carefully and allow one pound of sugar to every pint of juice. Heat the juice before adding the sugar until dissolved. Boil quickly for ten minutes, then bruise the bunch of mint and suspend it in the boiling jelly until the mint discolours. This will take about ten minutes. Test for setting by putting a little on a cold plate and allow to cool before potting.

Finely chopped mint may be added just before removing from the fire and a little edible green colouring before cooling.

Pickled Onions

This is a family recipe and the only one I have found that retains the flavour of the onions and keeps them crisp and hard. They should be eaten within six months or they will go soft.

small pickling onions	*sugar*
black pepper	*malt vinegar*

Choose small round pickling onions. Skin them and fill the jars, earthenware or glass, as they are prepared. Shake the jar from time to time so that the onions settle without too many gaps. When the jars are well filled, shake a fair amount of black pepper into each jar, using about one teaspoon of pepper to each two-pound jar of onions. Add one teaspoon of sugar and fill to the top with malt vinegar. Rock the jars to distribute the pepper and sugar, and seal. Keep in a cool place for three weeks before using.

Pickled Peaches

The recipe as given is for pickled peaches but plums, damsons, pears or green figs will do as well. The fruit should be rather under-ripe.

4 *lb. peaches*	½ *teaspoon salt*
1 *pint white wine vinegar*	1 *or 2 sticks cinnamon*
¾ *lb. sugar*	½ *oz. cloves*

Wipe the fruit, especially if using peaches, to remove the down. Prick the fruit all over with a needle and put into a large bowl. Boil the vinegar with the sugar and salt for fifteen minutes and pour over the fruit. Cover tightly and leave for twenty-four hours, then pour off the syrup and boil it for thirty minutes. Again, pour it over the fruit and leave until next day, as before. On the third day, tie the cinnamon and cloves in a muslin bag and boil together with the fruit and syrup. As soon as the contents of the pan bubble up and begin to rise remove from the fire and tip back into the bowl. When cold, put into jars and tie down tightly. Keep for two weeks before using.

Peach pickle is delicious, particularly with baked ham.

Aromatic Plums

3 *lb. black plums* or *damsons*
1 *heaped teaspoon powdered cloves*
1 *heaped teaspoon pimento*
1 *level teaspoon ground ginger*
1 *orange*
2 *lb. preserving sugar*
1½ *pints white wine vinegar*

Wash and prick with a fork three pounds of small under-ripe plums or damsons. Put them into a bowl with the powdered cloves, pimento and ground ginger, then grate in the peel of one orange. Dissolve the preserving sugar in the vinegar and pour over the plums. The bowl should be small enough for the liquor to cover the fruit completely. Leave overnight to marinate then strain off the liquid into a saucepan and boil for ten minutes before pouring it back into the bowl and leave overnight once more. Next day, turn the liquor and the plums into a preserving-pan and simmer very gently until the plums are soft but still whole. Draw away from the fire and let them cool before packing into warmed pots. Pour enough liquid into each pot to cover the fruit completely. Make the pots air-tight and store for at least two weeks before using. Delicious with hot or cold meats, particularly venison.

Plum Pickle

3 *lb. plums*
1 *lb. sour apples*
1 *lb. shallots*
2 *cloves garlic*
½ *lb. sultanas*
½ *oz. ground ginger*

1 teaspoon powdered
   cinnamon
1½ teaspoons salt

3 lb. demerara sugar
½ pint white wine vinegar

Stone the plums carefully. They should not be too ripe. Peel and quarter the apples. Skin the shallots and chop them up rather roughly. Slice the garlic cloves finely and put all together into a preserving-pan. Add the sultanas, ginger, cinnamon, salt, sugar and pour in the vinegar. Stir the contents of the pan well and bring to the boil. Simmer gently for about half an hour, stirring frequently, until the pickle thickens. When done, cool down and put into warmed pots. Seal well and keep for at least one month before using.

Green Tomato Chutney

For those fortunates who grow their own tomatoes out of doors or know someone who does, the following recipe is handy for using up the green tomatoes which develop too late in the year to ripen.

2 lb. green tomatoes
1 lb. cooking apples
½ lb. shallots
6 cloves garlic
¾ lb. brown sugar
1 lb. sultanas
1 flat teaspoon salt

½ teaspoon cayenne pepper
½ teaspoon ground ginger
½ teaspoon cardamom
½ teaspoon powdered
   cinnamon
¾ pint malt vinegar

Chop the tomatoes small, peel, core and slice the apples and put them together with the chopped shallots and sliced garlic cloves into the preserving-pan. Add the sugar, sultanas, seasoning and spices, mix well and stir in the vinegar. Place the pan over a low fire and bring slowly to the boil. Simmer gently until the chutney is dark and thick, about one hour. Let it cool in the pan and pot to keep.

Pickled Walnuts

brine (2 lb. common salt to	for each quart of vinegar:
2 quarts water)	1 *oz. allspice*
green walnuts	1 *oz. ground ginger*
	2 *oz. black peppercorns*

Prepare a strong brine allowing two pounds of common salt to two quarts of water. Choose young green walnuts and spear each one twice with the head of a darning needle. Put the walnuts into the brine and leave for nine days, changing the brine every three days. Drain the walnuts, put them on a large dish and dry them if possible in the sun for two or three days when they should be quite black. Put them into dry jars but do not quite fill the jars. Allow one ounce of allspice, one ounce of ground ginger and two ounces of black peppercorns to each quart of vinegar. Boil for ten minutes, then pour the hot strained vinegar over the walnuts which must be quite covered. Seal when cold and keep for one month before using. They will keep for two years if well sealed.

Spiced Vinegar for Pickles

$\frac{1}{4}$ *oz. cinnamon bark*	6 *peppercorns*
$\frac{1}{4}$ *oz. cloves*	1 *quart malt vinegar*
$\frac{1}{4}$ *oz. blade mace*	$\frac{1}{4}$ *oz. root ginger (if liked)*
$\frac{1}{4}$ *oz. allspice*	

Put the spices with the vinegar into a pan, cover and bring slowly to boiling point. Remove from the heat and infuse for at least two hours and preferably overnight. Strain the vinegar before using. If a hot pickle is liked add a quarter of an ounce of root ginger.

14. Preserves

Apricot Jam

4 *lb. apricots*   1 *lemon*
3 *lb. sugar* $\frac{1}{2}$ *pint water*
$\frac{1}{2}$ *oz. butter*   *salt*

Choose firm ripe fruit and split the apricots in half. Remove the stones and put them on one side. Lay the fruit in layers, alternating with the sugar, in an earthenware dish and leave covered for twenty-four hours. Next day put the fruit and sugar into a preserving-pan, add the water, and bring slowly to the boil. Crack a few of the stones and put the peeled kernels into the jam. Add the butter, a good pinch of salt and the juice of a lemon. Boil rapidly, stirring frequently until the jam sets and test by putting a little of the jam on a cold plate. If it is ready, a skin will form as the jam cools. Pour into warm jars and seal when the jam is cold.

Follow the same recipe for peach jam.

If fresh apricots are not available a good jam may be made from dried apricots when the method is slightly different.

1 *lb. dried apricots*   3 *lb. sugar*
3 *pints of water*   *salt*
1 *lemon*

Wash the apricots very thoroughly and put them to soak in the water for at least twenty-four hours. Next day put the apricots and the water in which they have been soaked into a preserving-pan and bring to the boil. Simmer gently for half an hour, then add the sugar, a good pinch of salt and the juice of the lemon. When the sugar is dissolved boil rapidly and stir almost constantly until the jam sets.

Black Currant Jam

> 4 *lb. black currants*   4 *lb. sugar*
> 2 *pints water*   ½ *teaspoon salt*

Wash the currants and remove the stalks. Put the fruit into a preserving-pan with the water and bring to the boil slowly. Simmer until the skins are tender and the liquid considerably reduced. This is important as the skins are usually very tough and will not soften once the sugar has been added. Add the sugar and salt and boil quickly for twenty minutes when the jam should jell when tested on a cold plate. Stir continuously after the sugar has been added to prevent the jam from burning. Pot and cover when cold.

Bramble Jelly

In the early autumn the hedgerows are full of luscious black fruit, and this is the time to make bramble jelly. Blackberries do not contain much pectin and will not set unless sour apples, lemon juice or an artificial setting agent are added. For a heavier set, use half sour apples, cut small with peel, and half blackberries.

> 4 *lb. blackberries* or *black-*   2 *tablespoons lemon juice if*
> *berries and apples* (*see*   *apples not used*
> *above*)   *sugar*
> ½ *pint water*

Wash the berries, which should not be over-ripe, and put them into a preserving-pan with the sour apples, if used, and water. Bring to the boil slowly, mashing the contents of the pan from time to time with a wooden spoon, and stew gently for about an hour. Remove from the fire and when cool strain through a jelly bag until all the juice is extracted. Measure the juice and allow one pound of sugar to each pint of juice. Put the juice back into the pan, add the sugar and stir until dissolved. Bring to the boil, add the lemon juice at this stage if apples have not been used, and boil briskly for fifteen or twenty minutes. Test for setting and as soon as it jells pour into warmed jars and leave to cool before covering.

Cherry Cordial

4 *lb. Morello cherries*   4 *lb. sugar*
2 *pints water*   *juice of* 1 *or* 2 *lemons*

Remove the stalks and stones from the cherries (there is a small tool specially made for removing stones) and put them in a preserving-pan with two pints of water and the stones tied in a muslin bag. If using a pressure cooker reduce the water by half a pint. Bring to the boil slowly and simmer until the fruit is soft. Add the sugar and dissolve it slowly then boil fast until rather syrupy. Allow to cool a little, then pour off the syrup into bottles and cork tightly. The remaining cherries may be potted and sealed and used with junket, yoghourt or as a rather runny jam. Children love the juice as a summer drink diluted with water.

Cherry Jam

4 *lb. Morello cherries*   1 *saltspoon salt*
4 *lb. sugar*   2 *tablespoons lemon juice*

Wash the cherries and remove the stalks and stones with a small tool specially made for the job. Stoning the cherries without it is murder! Put the stoned cherries into a heavy-bottomed pan with the stones tied in a muslin bag. Bring slowly to the boil and cook slowly for fifteen or twenty minutes, when the skins should be tender. Add the sugar and stir until dissolved. Add the salt and lemon juice and boil quickly until there is a light set on testing. Cool and pot and cover when quite cold.

Crab Apple Jelly

   crab apples or *crab apples*   *sugar*
      and damsons   *water*
  sprig of sweet-scented
    geranium

Siberian crab apples make the best jelly but are not so easy to come by these days. Equal quantities of crab apples and damsons make a delicious jelly and the flavour is further improved by putting a sprig of sweet-scented geranium in the first boiling. Rinse the fruit well in plenty of cold water but do not peel or core the apples. Put them into a large preserving-pan and allow one pint of cold water to each one and a half pounds of fruit. This should just cover the fruit in the pan. Bring to the boil and simmer gently until the fruit is soft and the goodness extracted, then pass through a jelly bag and leave to drip overnight. Do not squeeze the bag or the jelly will be cloudy. Next day, measure the liquid and pour it back into the preserving-pan. Bring to the boil once more and boil rapidly for five or ten minutes, removing any scum which may rise to the surface. This ensures a clear jelly. Add three-quarters of a pound of sugar to each pint of juice, heat slowly and stir until the sugar has dissolved. Boil rapidly for half an hour, then test for setting. A spoonful on a cold plate will jell if it is ready. Allow to cool a little before pouring into warmed jars and seal down when cold. This jelly keeps well.

Cranberry Jam

4 *lb. cranberries*	*water*
4 *lb. sugar*	1 *lemon*
pinch of salt	

Wash the berries and put them into a heavy saucepan and just enough water to cover them. Simmer slowly until the berries are soft then add the sugar and a pinch of salt. Stir until the sugar has dissolved then add the strained juice of a large lemon and boil rapidly until the jam reaches setting point. Remove from the fire and allow to cool a little before putting into warmed jars. Cover when cold. A leaf or two of sweet-scented geranium improves the flavour enormously.

Cranberry Jelly

cranberries	*sugar*
water	2 *or* 3 *leaves of sweet-scented*
pinch of salt	*geranium*

Wash and pick over the cranberries removing any over-ripe ones. Put the berries into a heavy saucepan, barely cover with cold water, add a pinch of salt and the geranium leaves. Stew gently until the fruit is quite soft and pulpy. Cool for ten minutes then strain overnight through a jelly bag or a piece of fine muslin. Next day, measure the juice and return to the pan allowing one pound of sugar to one pint of juice. Stir until the sugar is dissolved then boil rapidly until setting point is reached. Remove the scum which rises to the surface if granulated sugar is used instead of preserving sugar. It should jell within half an hour. When cooled, pour into warmed jars and cover when cold. If the cranberries are rather ripe, add the juice of a lemon to aid the setting of the jelly.

Damson Cheese

damsons   *sugar*
½ *teacup water*

Pick the stalks from the fruit, wash them well and put into a preserving-pan with half a teacup of water. Simmer until the damsons are soft, and remove the stones as they rise to the surface. Beat the fruit through a coarse sieve and weigh the pulp. Allow one pound of sugar to each pound of pulp, and put into a preserving-pan. Simmer slowly for half an hour, stirring frequently. Skim well and boil fast for another half hour or until the preserve looks firm. Put it into pots and seal. A few damson kernels added to the cheese improves the flavour.

Lemon Cheese

3 *lemons*   3 *eggs*
8 *oz. sugar*   *salt*
4 *oz. butter*

Wash the lemons and grate the rinds finely. Squeeze the juice from the lemons and put into a heavy saucepan with the butter, grated rind, sugar and a pinch of salt. When the sugar and butter have melted, add the very well-beaten eggs and stir continuously with a wooden spoon until the cheese thickens and coats the spoon. Remove from the fire and allow to cool a little before potting. This method takes about ten minutes to cook but it will not keep for more than two weeks.

Lemon Curd

8 *oz. sugar*   3 *lemons*
4 *oz. butter*   3 *eggs*

Melt the sugar and butter together in a double saucepan. Add the grated rind and juice of the lemons and stir until thoroughly combined. Allow to cool a little, then add the well-beaten eggs, stir well and cook over a low flame until the mixture thickens. Remove from the fire and pour into warmed pots to keep. Seal when cold.

Marmalade

2 *lb. Seville oranges*   6 *lb. preserving sugar*
1 *lemon*   1 *teaspoon salt*
6 *pints water*

Wash the oranges and lemon, cut them in half and squeeze out the juice. Remove the pips and as much of the pith and membrane as will come away easily and tie them firmly in a muslin bag. Slice the peel to the desired thickness with a very sharp knife; a marmalade cutter is a great time saver but it cuts finely and for thick marmalade a knife has to be used. Put the fruit, juice and bag of pith and pips into a large bowl. Add the water and leave to steep overnight. Next day, pour the contents of the bowl into a preserving pan and boil until the rind is tender and the liquid reduced by about one-third. This should take about one hour and a half. Remove the bag of pips and squeeze it as dry of juice as possible into the pan. Add the salt and sugar, stir until it is dissolved, then boil briskly until the marmalade jells. Pot and leave to cool and cover tightly to keep.

Medlar Jelly (1840)

3 *lb. medlars*   1 *quart water*
sugar

Put the medlars, which should be soft, into a preserving-pan and barely cover with water, using one quart of water to three pounds of medlars. Simmer until the fruit is soft. Mash well with a wooden spoon and strain overnight through a jelly bag. Put the juice into a preserving-pan and boil fast for half an hour. Remove from the fire, add the sugar, allowing one pound to each pint of juice, and then stir over a low fire until the sugar is dissolved. Skim well and boil quickly for twenty minutes when it should be ready for potting. Seal when cold.

Mincemeat

1½ lb. cooking apples	1 orange
1 lb. suet	1 lemon
½ lb. raisins	1 tangerine
1 lb. currants	1 teaspoon ground ginger
1 lb. sultanas	1 teaspoon cinnamon
4 oz. mixed peel	1 teaspoon ground nutmeg
4 oz. almonds	1 small wineglass brandy
¾ lb. moist brown sugar	1 small wineglass rum

Peel, core and quarter the apples. Clean and shred the suet. Clean the dried fruit and remove the skin from the almonds by steeping them in boiling water for a few minutes; the skin will then slip off easily when rubbed between the finger and thumb. Put the apples, suet, mixed fruit, peel and almonds through a mincer and into a large mixing-bowl. Add the grated rind and juice of the orange, lemon and tangerine with the sugar and spices and stir thoroughly until well mixed. Add the brandy and rum, stir well, cover and leave in a cool place for two days, then pack tightly into clean dry jars and seal.

The mincemeat should be kept for at least one month before using and will keep longer if more brandy is added and the jars are well sealed.

Orange Jelly

2 *lb. sweet oranges*   2 *lb. Seville oranges*
2 *lemons*   *pinch of salt*
sugar

Use two pounds of sweet juicy oranges, two pounds of Seville
oranges and two lemons. Cut them up small and put them into
a preserving-pan, pips and all. Cover with cold water and
cook slowly until the peel is soft. Strain through a jelly bag
overnight but do not squeeze the bag or the jelly may be
cloudy. Measure the juice and add one pound of sugar to
each pint of juice. Pour back into the pan, add the sugar and
a good pinch of salt. Bring to the boil slowly, stirring to dissolve the sugar. Boil rapidly for about fifteen minutes and test
for setting. Pour into hot jars and cover when cold.

Plum and Apple Jelly

Victoria plums   *sugar*
cooking apples   1 *lemon*
water

Put equal quantities of ripe Victoria plums and quartered
sour cooking apples, peel and all, into a preserving-pan. Cover
with cold water and bring to the boil slowly. Simmer gently
until the fruit is soft and pulpy and strain through a jelly
bag overnight. To each pint of strained juice add one pound
of sugar and bring to the boil slowly, stirring until the sugar
is dissolved. Add the juice of a large lemon and boil briskly
for about fifteen minutes until a little dropped on a cold plate
sets quickly, when a skin should form. Cool before pouring
into heated jars and seal well.

Plum Jam

plums
sugar

water (if required)
pinch of salt

Allow one pound of sugar to each pound of fruit. Split the plums in half, remove the stones and lay the fruit in layers with sugar on a suitable dish. Leave for twenty-four hours in a warm place. Some plums run a fair amount of juice while others do not and in this case add a teacupful of water. Put the fruit into a preserving-pan, add a pinch of salt and bring slowly to the boil. Simmer very gently for about half an hour, then boil rapidly for fifteen minutes, stirring constantly, and remove the scum as it rises to keep the jam clear. Allow to cool a little and pot. If some of the stones are cracked and the kernels added to the jam just before it is ready the flavour is much improved.

Quince Jam

2 *lb. quince*
2¼ *lb. sugar*
2 *oz. almonds*
1 *pod vanilla*
water

1 *sprig sweet basil*
1 *sprig sweet-scented geranium*
juice of 1 *lemon*
salt

Wash and peel the quince, slice them finely and put them into a preserving-pan with the lemon juice and a pinch of salt. Barely cover with water and simmer gently about one hour when the fruit should be soft. Add the sugar and peeled almonds and stir until the sugar has dissolved. Boil fast for twenty minutes adding the vanilla, sweet basil and geranium ten minutes before removing from the fire. When setting point is reached, allow to cool, remove the herbs and vanilla, and pour the jam into warmed jars. Seal when cold.

Quince Jelly

2 *lb. quince*
3 *pints water*
salt
1 *pod vanilla*
1 *sprig sweet basil*

1 *sprig sweet-scented geranium*
sugar
juice of 1 *lemon*

Wipe and cut the quince into quarters without peeling them and throw them at once into a bowl of cold salted water to prevent them from discolouring. Put the fruit into a preserving-pan with the vanilla pod, sweet basil and geranium leaves. Add a pinch of salt and cover with water. Bring to the boil and simmer slowly until the fruit is soft. Remove from the fire and when cool enough to handle drain through a jelly bag overnight.

Measure the juice and allow one pound of sugar to each pint of juice. Put the juice into a preserving-pan and heat before adding the sugar. Stir until the sugar is dissolved, add the lemon juice and boil rapidly for twenty minutes until setting point. Allow to cool a little, pot and seal when cold. If liked, a few peeled almonds may be added.

Raspberry Jam

3 *lb. raspberries*
3 *lb. sugar*

1 *teacup red currant juice* or *juice of one lemon*
pinch of salt

Wash the raspberries, remove the stalks and put the fruit into a preserving-pan over a low fire. Bring slowly to the boil, breaking the fruit and stirring with a wooden spoon. Boil for fifteen minutes before adding the sugar, salt and, if available, a cup of redcurrant juice which much improves the flavour. If currant juice is used, omit the lemon juice. Boil rapidly for fifteen or twenty minutes, stirring frequently and skimming if necessary. Test for setting on a cold plate and cool before pouring into warmed jars. Seal when cold.

Red Currant Jelly

3 *lb. red currants*	*sugar*
¾ *pint water*	*salt*
2 *sticks cinnamon*	

Wash the fruit well, remove any leaves but leave the fruit on the stalks, and put into a preserving-pan with the water and the sticks of cinnamon. Place the pan over a low fire and bring to the boil slowly, mashing the fruit with a wooden spoon. Simmer gently until the fruit is cooked and all the berries are thoroughly pulped. Strain through a jelly bag and let it drip for several hours, preferably overnight. Measure the extract, pour back into the preserving-pan and bring to the boil. Skim if necessary, and add one pound of sugar to each pint of juice, and a pinch of salt. Stir to dissolve the sugar then boil briskly for about fifteen minutes and test for jelling. Allow to cool a little before pouring into warmed jars and seal well.

Strawberry Jam

strawberries	*lemons*
sugar	*salt*

It is important that whole unbruised fruit is used or the jam will not keep. The addition of lemon juice helps the jam to set and is much nicer than tartaric acid or other pectin aids.

To each pound of fruit allow one pound of sugar, the juice of one lemon and half a teaspoon of salt.

Hull the berries, wash them well and put them into a heavy-bottomed preserving-pan over a low fire. Add the juice and pulp of the lemons but not the pith or pips. Stew gently until the fruit is soft. It is better to shake the pan from time to time rather than stir with a wooden spoon at this stage of cooking to keep the fruit whole. Add the sugar and salt and boil briskly until the preserve sets. Once the sugar has dissolved and come to boiling point the fruit will not disintegrate and it is safe to stir the jam. Test for setting by putting a spoonful on a cold plate. As it cools a skin should form and the jam set. Remove the pan from the fire and allow to cool before pouring into warmed clean pots. Seal when quite cold.

Index